Beautifully Broken

Illuminate in Your Brokenness

Psalm 34:18

Cheri Gable

Copyright © 2017 Cheri Gable

Front cover art work credits and rights to Meganbcreative@gmail.com and thecolormaryann@gmail.com

All rights reserved.

ISBN: 9780578647180

DEDICATION

To all of God's broken and lost kids

ACKNOWLEDGMENTS

Thank you to all the pastors that have invested in me, fed me, furthered me and even failed me. Thank you to all my family and friends that have supported me, encouraged me, furthered me and even left me. Thank you to all of God's lost kids that desire change, don't know that change exists and those who are in the midst of change. You are why I had the courage to write this book.

CONTENTS

Introduction	ii
1 Recognize the Beauty in Broken	1
2 Recall the Moments	13
3 Revive the Heart	27
4 Receive the Fountains of Grace	45
5 Respond to the Strip Down	61
6 Realign	73
7 Rearm	89
8 Reciprocate the Illumination	105

BEAUTIFULLY BROKEN

INTRODUCTION

"The Lord is close to the brokenhearted and saves those who are crushed in spirit." Psalm 34:18

This book is an interactive process that was formed out of my own journey of walking through a season of being beautifully broken. As I cried out for others on the same journey, this book began to take form. There are times and seasons for everything. *Ecclesiastes 3:1-8 (NIV) "There is a time for everything, and a season for every activity under the heavens: a time to be born and a time to die, a time to plant and a time to uproot, a time to kill and heal, a time to tear down and build up, a time to weep and a time to laugh, a time to mourn and a time to dance, a time to scatter stones and a time to gather them, a time to embrace and a time to refrain from embracing, a time to search and a time to give up, a time to keep and a time to throw away, a time to tear and a time to mend, a time to be silent and a time to speak, a time to love and a time to hate, a time for war and a time for peace."*

As you read this book, know that it is time for you to heal and stop killing yourself and others with your broken life. The greatness of what is in this book can only happen when you surrender to every aspect of it with honesty and completeness. Are you ready? If the answer is yes, prepare yourself for change!

In this book there are eight steps that will guide you on a journey to illuminate amid your dark seconds, moments, hours and years. Each step of this journey will build upon the previous step. Below are the sections that will be used throughout each step as a tool to help you navigate through to the victory your heart is crying out for.

AFRESH WORD

Proverbs 18:21(NIV) "The tongue has the power of life and death, and those who love it will eat its fruit."

Words are so powerful they can refresh, or they can deplete, hurt or heal, encourage or discourage. This section of each chapter will bring a word to encourage and bring life to you in the midst of all brokenness. Afresh means in a new or different way. It will help you to view things with a new and different perspective. This will be done by the presentation of life experiences and stories from the Bible. These stories will help you to dedicate yourself to the process and help you to see any areas of denial that may be blinding you and keeping you bound in a life of anger, bitterness, closed emotions, negativity, loneliness, and destruction.

REALITY RECALL

Revelation 12:11(KJV) "And they overcame him by the blood of the Lamb, and by the word of their testimony, and they loved not their lives unto the death."

The second section of each chapter is titled Reality Recall. This section consists of a real-life experience from someone of today. The stories shared will be used to bring hope, share grace, provide encouragement, display love, and help you to see that you are not alone. The section in return will lead you to the understanding that we are all *beautifully broken,* and that greatness can come from all situations.

MEDITATION MOMENT

John 8:32 (NIV) "Then you should know the truth, and the truth will set you free."

In the Meditation Moment, there will be an opportunity for you to be still, pray, worship and read a Bible story that will correlate with the step in the chapter. It is important to realize that Jesus is the source of all eyes being open to the true reality of freedom, understanding, and forward motion. It is imperative that you do not pass this section up or just skim through it. Get a Bible out, look up every scripture, pray the prayers, listen to worship and be still in the moment with God. You may have to rise earlier or stay up a little later. The freedom you will receive will outweigh any of the sacrifices you have to make.

LINK LEVERAGE

James 5:16 "Therefore confess your sins to each other and pray for each other so that you may be healed. The prayer of a righteous man is powerful and effective."

Rewarding relationships are the key to success in the *Beautifully Broken* process. It is imperative that you connect with someone who can help you walk this journey to illumination. This journey is almost impossible to walk alone. For this reason, a link partner is suggested or even required to receive the fullness of this journey. A link partner is someone that you will ask to read and walk through this book with you. You will encourage one another, challenge one another and love one another enough to be honest and open with each other. The link partner will help you grow into the person God desires for you to be. People that are not afraid to be vulnerable, trust and love again.

It is important for you to commit to the development and growth of the link partner that mutually agrees to this journey. You cannot quit halfway through. In brokenness one of the fears is that you are not good enough and people will leave you when they know the true you. Squash this lie by staying committed to one another for the entire journey.

Listening is a key to healthy development and success as a link partner. To know how to be a better listener look at the ideas presented in the book *"Listening, the Forgotten Skill"* by Madelyn Burley-Allen. It states that there are three levels of listening.

Level 1: Listening nonjudgmentally with the understanding of the intent and feelings, paying attention to the speaker's total communication, and processing what is being said verbally and nonverbally.

Level 2: Hearing words but not making the effort to understand the speaker's intent, appearing to listen intently when in fact only slightly concentrating.

Level 3: Listening in spurts, more hearing going on than listening; being passive or judgmental.

Level one is the level of listening that we need to consistently strive to reach to be effective in helping people out in general. It will produce respect, trust, rapport, self-esteem, decreased misunderstanding, increased productivity and retention of information gathered. Depth will come into your relationships when you learn to listen with intent. It opens avenues of trust and respect that will set the stage for the rest of the journey through this book.

Your link partner will present you with accountability. Accountability is taking responsibility for your actions or the lack thereof. The Link Leverage is a tool that the link partner will use to hold you accountable for specific struggles, goals and action plans to help you to grow. You will fill this out each week and share it with your link partner. This tool will help you to focus on forward motion always. It will also be a very valuable resource to look back on and see the growth and advancement from week to week.

See the next page for the Link Leverage tool that you should fill out at the end of each chapter.

LINK LEVERAGE TOOL

AWARENESS
- Write three words that stood out to you while reading this chapter.

ASK
- Ask yourself what did these words speak to you?

GOAL
- Write down one goal that will help you to grow this week.

CHANGE
- What change can you make to acheive your goal?

SERVE
- Who did I serve this week and how did it make me feel?

ILLUMINATION

Matthew 5:14-16 (NIV) "You are the light of the world. A town built on a hill cannot be hidden. Neither do people light a lamp and put it under a bowl. Instead, they put it on its stand, and it gives light to everyone in the house. In the same way, let your light shine before others, that they may see your good deeds and praise your father in heaven."

Now it is time to reflect on what value you received from the chapter. Another important piece of recognizing beauty in broken is to think about what you will do with the value you have received. Think of it like this, ladies: You have a diamond given to you. Would you take this diamond and look at it for a bit and then throw it away? This diamond is better if you use it and put it on something that you can see daily. Gentlemen: Diamonds might not be your thing. You may view it as a valuable ticket for a front row seat of a championship game with your favorite team. You get the ticket, look at it, and throw it away. Either way, you are missing out on the value of what you have received. The information that you will get weekly will be worth more than either of these items and will be worth doing something with. It is always important to reflect on what you learn in each chapter and give God thanks for your wins.

Use this journal time to write three valuable nuggets of what you have learned and how you have won in life because of them. Then write three things you are thankful for.

SALVATION

If you have never received the friendship and the love that God displayed on the cross, I want you to understand that it is all on your terms. It will not be forced on you while reading this book. However, this book is full of Jesus. Maybe you have never even been introduced to who Jesus is and how He can benefit you in your life.

You might be asking yourself, "Who is this Jesus?" His character is one of greatness and love. These verses will help you to see who He is:

- **He is full of sweetness and is desirable:**
  Song of Songs 5:16 *(NIV)*
  "His mouth is sweetness itself; he is altogether lovely. This is my beloved, this is my friend, daughters of Jerusalem."

- **He is holy and true:**
  Revelation 3:7 *(NIV)*
  "To the angel of the church in Philadelphia write: These are the words of him who is holy and true, who holds the keys of David. What he opens no one can shut, and what he shuts no one can open."

- **He is faithful:**
  1 Thessalonians 5:24 *(NIV)*
  "The one who calls you is faithful, and he will do it."

- **He is full of grace and truth:**
  John 1:14 *(NIV)*
  "The Word became flesh and made his dwelling among us. We have seen his glory, the glory of the one and only Son, who came from the Father, full of grace and truth."

- **He is humble:**
  Philippians 2:8 *(NIV)*
  "And being found in appearance as a man, he humbled himself by becoming obedient to death, even death on a cross."

- **He is full of hope, joy, and peace:**
  Romans 15:13 *(NIV)*
  "May the God of hope fill you with all joy and peace as you trust in him, so that you may overflow with hope by the power of the Holy Spirit."

- **ABOVE ALL, HIS LOVE IS REAL AND FOREVER:**
  Romans 8:37-39 (NIV)
  "No, in all these things, we are more than conquerors through him who loved us. For I am convinced that neither death nor life, neither angels nor demons, neither the present nor the future, nor any powers, neither height nor depth, nor anything else in all creation, will be able to separate us from the love of God that is in Christ Jesus our Lord."

If your heart does begin to desire a friendship with Jesus, it is as simple as talking to Him about a few things. Romans 10:9 *(NIV)* says *"For, if you confess with your mouth that Jesus is Lord and believe in your heart that God raised him from the dead, you will be saved."* It also says in Acts 3:19 *(NIV)* *"Repent, then, and turn to God, so that your sins may be wiped out, that times of refreshing may come from the Lord."*

What exactly is repenting? The definition is to turn from sin and dedicate oneself to the amendment of one's life. Sin is anything that would separate you from God. The idea is to turn your back on sin and go a different direction. The new direction will be to the cross—to JESUS.

When trying to figure out what sin is you should read Galatians 5:19-21 *(NIV) "The acts of the flesh are obvious: sexual immorality, impurity, and debauchery; idolatry and witchcraft; hatred, discord, jealousy, fits of rage, selfish ambition, dissensions, factions, and envy; drunkenness, orgies, and the like. I warn you like I did before, that those who live like this will not inherit the kingdom of God."*

The opposite of this is a life in the spirit found in Galatians 5:22-24 *(NIV) "But the fruit of the Spirit is love, joy, peace, forbearance, kindness, goodness, faithfulness, gentleness, and self-control. Against such things, there is no law. Those who belong to Christ Jesus have crucified the flesh with its passions and desires."*
Take some time to evaluate which side you are on. Are you on the side of the flesh or the side of the Spirit? When you evaluate, don't evaluate to condemn—evaluate to bring life and freedom. Romans

8 (NIV) will help you to understand this, *"Therefore, there is now no condemnation for those who are in Christ Jesus, because through Christ Jesus the law of the Spirit who gives life has set you free from the law of sin and death."*

If you would like to enter a friendship with Jesus, just pray a confession of your heart to him now and you shall be saved.

Jesus, I believe in my heart that you are Lord and that God raised you from the dead on the third day. Please forgive me for my sins, wrong things I have done, and help me to turn from those bad things and live a life for you. Thank you for being a new best friend that will never leave me—one that I can count on and live with forever. Thank you for the great love you have for me. In Jesus' name, amen.

Welcome to the family! I would suggest that you write the day, time and the story of what brought you to this decision. Do this so you will never forget this moment because it will change your life forever. Your story will someday help someone else to commit to a friendship with Jesus too.

Date _____ Time _____ Location_____
Story:
_____
_____
_____

One thing to remember is what it says in Romans 3:23 *(NIV)* *"For all have sinned and fallen short of the glory of God."* Just because you have said this prayer doesn't mean you will not choose to do wrong again, as we all fall short occasionally. The Bible does say in James 4:7 *"Submit yourselves, then, to God. Resist the devil, and he will flee from you."*

In the Hebrew language, every letter has a meaning and a numeric value. This creates relevancy to each number. The Hebrew meaning of the number eight represents a new life or new beginning, meaning a new classification or creation. This book is eight chapters for this specific reason.

As you read and complete the steps in this book view it as a new beginning for you in life. 2 Corinthians 5:17 *(NIV) "Therefore, if anyone is in Christ, the new creation has come: The old has gone, the new is here!"* 2 Corinthians 4:6-10 *(NIV)* states that, *"For God, who said, 'Let light shine out of darkness,' made his light shine in our hearts to give us the light of the knowledge of God's glory displayed in the face of Christ. But we have this treasure in jars of clay to show that this all-surpassing power is from God and not from us. We are hard pressed on every side, but not crushed; perplexed, but not in despair; persecuted, but not abandoned; struck down, but not destroyed. We always carry around in our body the death of Jesus, so that the life of Jesus may also be revealed in our body."*

It is time to allow God to create a new light in your life so that you can shine. Allow him to remove all debris and produce in you a clean and pure love for Him, yourself and others. It is time to Illuminate! Let's go…

Beautifully Broken

Broken in pieces,
I have failed once again.
A battle with the devil, a fight with myself... It feels like
I can never win. My mistakes bring me guilt, my guilt
causes pain.
I am separated from God!
My sin brings me shame.
How dare I speak his name? He knows me too well.
A prisoner of my thoughts, I am trapped in a cell.
How will I escape? Who will love me like this?
With the wrong, I have done.
I feel my rights don't exist!
But wait...
There is a man named Jesus,
Who died on the cross Who took up my
sins and paid His life as the cost. He tells
me "you are beautiful." because His love
made me clean. He knew the wrong I
would do, But He still chose me.
Only when I am empty,
Can God fill my soul, And only when
I am broken, Can God make me
whole?

By Tamera Brown

BEAUTIFULLY BROKEN

STEP 1
RECOGNIZE THE BEAUTY IN BROKEN

"Rise above the destruction of yesterday into the beauty of a new day."

AFRESH WORD

We have all experienced it at one point in our lives if we are living: BROKENNESS. Brokenness is brought on by many circumstances, such as broken relationships, unhealthy emotions, financial concerns, death, disease, addiction and a plethora of other circumstances. Just fill in this blank with whatever situation that has brought on your brokenness _____. The situations are endless because we live in a world full of brokenness. The first to being Beautifully Broken is realizing that great beauty can be discovered in the middle of what seems like your darkest day.

Our perspective on broken "things" is that they are bad and of no use anymore. They normally make their way to the trash to be destroyed and put out of our sight and space. Our landfills are full of broken things, things that have been thrown out due to their original state being altered by wear and tear or accidents. What use is something if it is broken, right?

This is how I viewed my own broken life—many people had thrown me out. I thought, *how can I be worth anything to anyone, including Jesus and my destiny*? I had taken on a mentality of shame and unworthiness. This is all I thought my life consisted of in the past, present and for the future.

There are so many lenses that we can choose to view our life through. Yes, we choose. We don't choose our situations all the time, but we do choose our lenses. I often ask myself: With what lens am I viewing my own life? Is it a lens of unworthiness, a dark lens, a dirty lens or a lens of beauty? The lens we view our brokenness through will determine how we see our situation. Do we see it as a growth point? Do we see it as a life point? Do we see it as a dead point? Are you looking through the dirty lens that tells you lies and blinds you from seeing the beauty and the purpose that your brokenness will produce? Is your view distorted through a fog of pain or are you viewing through the clear lens of Christ? This lens will cause you to see your situation clearly and with purity of heart and mind. So, ask yourself: What lens am I viewing my situation through? When you think of your situation what are the six keywords that come to your mind?

_____

_____

Can you see any good coming from your situation?

_____

    This interactive book is a product of my journey when I began to view my situation through the lens of Christ. Part of viewing through this lens was recognizing that there will always be broken moments in my life. Whether these moments are viewed as a mess or as beautiful will determine my victory or failure. It is imperative to see that through our damaged hearts and souls can come great victory. One of God's greatest promises is that He will heal the brokenhearted. It says in Psalm 34:18 (NIV) *"The Lord is close to the brokenhearted and saves those who are crushed in spirit."* There is the gift of hope wrapped up for all of us in this one promise.

    If you feel broken, realize that there is beauty in your brokenness, and you are not alone. I know initially that I did not see the beauty, I was only able to see the brokenness. I was in a spot of feeling hopeless and like I had no life left in me. It is in this spot that I found the vision for my future. On the floor in my bedroom in Greenwood, Indiana, as I cried out to God in despair, I heard His voice say, "You are beautifully broken, and you are mine." I said back to God, "Beauty and broken do not go together." My thought was beauty is, well, beautiful. "God how can these two intertwine at all?" I asked. As I asked God this question, He drew me to his word in 2 Corinthians 12:9 (NIV). Nestled in the middle of that scripture I found life, *"...power is made perfect in weakness..."* LIFE, LIFE, LIFE! There is power in all my weak moments!

    His reply was in a vision of two vases, one shattered and put back together and one completely whole never being damaged. In the vision of those two vases, God inserted a light. The broken vase began to show me that it is in our broken places that His light will shine through us to the world. It was at that moment that I truly understood that the broken messes in our lives are what makes us so beautiful in God's eyes. He never expected perfection from anyone of us, so why do we expect it for and from ourselves? He takes ashes and makes them into something beautiful. He took dirt and created the beauty of humanity. He can take our brokenness and change the world.

On the flip side of that vision, there was a whole vase that was closed and dark. The vase did not present any light to anyone, it just held it all inside. We all have Jesus, who created us, and lives in us, even in the darkness of our lives. It is just a matter of a surrendering our will to Him and allowing him to create a flow of His light from our lives to others. If we keep ourselves closed, acting like we have no cracks, it will create negative thoughts and emotions. Those thoughts will then create a journey down a dark path full of destructive behaviors.

When we have negative thoughts and emotions it does not just affect us, it permeates out of us into the world. It will bring darkness to a world that is in desperate need of the light. Darkness may look like anger, unforgiveness, guilt, shame, condemnation, jealousy, envy… this list could go on and on. Negativity and brokenness are what I was presenting to the world in my dark place, all because I could not see that in my weakness, strength could be found.

How this lack of light affects us, and others could be compared with a car driving with no head lights in the pitch black, dark country night. We are driving along with no thought of where we are heading and no idea of what is in front of us. Other cars cannot see where we are or where we are heading. They do not know how much space to allow for your passing or how quickly you are approaching. The darkness can cause great confusion and even death. You are killing people with your darkness. It is time to illuminate by realizing that all things can be made new.

Each person will walk out their unique moments in life in ways that will bring beauty or darkness to the world. If we view the cracks as useful, we can bring beauty and light to all who see it.

Beauty is found in the light. It is this light that will drown out all the darkness.

Many people, including myself, view a broken vase as something that we need to get rid of because we struggle to see the beauty in the future of that brokenness. We need to remember that we are all a bunch of fragmented pieces that are being put back together continuously by the flow from the cross, the Maker's hand. The flow from the cross is what will bring life to everyone who accepts it in the end. Are you allowing the flow from the cross to clean your viewing lens of life so that you can see clearly with beauty and strength?

REALITY RECALL

By Cheri Gable

This is my recall: I looked around at every avenue of my life, and all I could see was brokenness. Broken relationships, broken finances, broken covenants, brokenness all around. My fragmented pieces caused me to view my life as a pile of broken moments that mounted up all around me. This mountain of destruction that I sat in the middle of was the only thing I could be or become. I desperately needed to be thrown out so that I would not have to deal with the pain of my life any longer. I wanted to soak myself in the heap of rubble, because I didn't feel worthy of anything else. So, I sat surrounded by the darkness.

The darkness of a broken marriage. I had been married for 20 years. For 11 of those years, my now ex-husband had been choosing other things over me—mainly pornography, which in my eyes, he was choosing other women. We sought counsel on multiple occasions, as "divorced" was not the box that I wanted to check on the marital status question. However, my heart could not take any more. After many broken promises and much heartbreak, I went to my pastor to seek counsel for a divorce.

In November of 2013, it was final. I walked into the courtroom and sat beside my husband for the last time. He is a good man, but the continual heartbreak had become too much for me. It stole from me, my fight, my love, and my devotion. Divorce was one of the hardest decisions I have ever had to make in my life. It created in me a sense of not being enough. I wasn't enough to keep my husband from choosing the other woman over me.

This moment of feeling like I wasn't enough created an opportunity for the devil to swoop in and create other situations in my life that would cause me to continue to view myself as unworthy. He knew that if he kept me in this moment of unworthiness that I would discount and disconnect myself from the call of God on my life. He knew if he could keep me in the false view of brokenness that I would not see the greatness of the One living in me. I wanted my marriage to work. I wanted him to love me enough to stop the madness. The lack of commitment to stop caused a great amount of brokenness in my life.

Then came this unexpected separation from my spiritual father. Church hurt—this is a hurt that can destroy you because it is not what you expect to happen in the church. I was at the church for 18 years and highly involved. Youth and Children's Pastor was a title that I carried for 13 of those years. This church was a place where I sacrificed my life for the cause of Christ. Through much prayer, counsel, and fasting, I felt God calling me to Florida to invest in the youth and children of West Palm Beach. However, this did not go over very well, and my pastor thought I was in rebellion. There were meetings before elders, other leaders and the entire congregation where I was presented as a failure and unworthy in front of hundreds of people. This created a great amount of brokenness in my life.

I thought that he would be excited that God wanted me to take what he had imparted to me and invest in another church and location. I left that church and Indiana devastated. Again, this pastor is a great man. I know that he loved me and did not want to see me leave. I had given my heart to the Lord in his church, and I was his spiritual daughter.

I moved to Florida in March of 2014 with an extensive amount of brokenness from my past. Not realizing the depth of my pain, I began to pour it out on others. The church that moved me to Florida had great expectations, excitement, and enthusiasm for what God was going to do through me in the church.

When you are broken without realizing that you are beautiful, you will begin to throw that brokenness on others hoping that it will leave you. This is exactly what I did. I didn't even realize at the time that I was deeply wounding others with my display. I had the mask of everything being ok on and refused to talk to anyone or even acknowledge that I was hurting. Through this lack of acknowledgment and focus on the beauty, I hurt an entire community with my decisions after I arrived.

I met a man and let him woo me into his mind games and away from my call and my purpose in Florida. I was not even at the church for a full year before I left. I quickly fell into an unhealthy relationship and pursued it instead of God. One month into this madness, the conviction, guilt, and shame of my choices began to set in. I moved back to Indiana to find myself and God again. This man consistently pursued me from thousands of miles away. He gave me a false sense of worthiness because of the pursuit. The passionate pursuit made it extremely hard to disconnect from him even though I knew he was not the reward God had in store for me.

As I sat lost in the mountain of fragmented pieces, feeling like there was no way out, I began to search. I read God's word, and it created in me a desire to walk in faith again. I had stopped all communication with God because I felt like He could not hear me through the rubble. I started to talk to Him again, and I said, "God I know I have screwed up, I have walked away from you, but if you could help me find my way back to you, I would appreciate it." While I talked to God, I said, "If this man is not for me, please remove me from his heart and cause him to lose his desire to pursue me." Within 24 hours the man called me and said that he had found someone else and was going to cut all communication with me from that point on. He ended up marrying the other woman six weeks after we officially ended our relationship. What I felt at that point was this love was yet another hiding spot for my brokenness.

Even though I prayed this prayer and wanted desperately to be in the flow of where God wanted me to be, this phone call crushed me. I felt like even the one that was pursuing me with intensity had abandoned me and threw me out with the trash. Another setback. I kept searching for "someone" to choose me for life and make me feel worthy. All along God was choosing me, but I was refusing Him. I refused the one that would hold me tight and never let me go. I refused the one I could trust. I refused the one true love.

I don't tell you these stories to disparage any one of the individuals involved, including myself. Telling these stories is part of the journey that I am traveling on with God to the recovery of my life and my calling. The enemy tries to get us in a spot of paralyzation by brokenness, but I refused to remain there any longer. My heart's cry is that as you read this book, you will refuse also.

The enemy tries to put us in the zone of brokenness so that we will not produce beauty for the kingdom. When you allow yourself to die in the middle of failure and fragments, there will be a lot of regret, condemnation, and sadness. Rise above the destruction of your yesterday into the beauty of a new day.

MEDITATION MOMENT

STILL MOMENTS

Be still in God's presence for a few minutes and think about your brokenness and let God help you to see what lens you are looking at life through.

PRAYER
God,

Open my eyes to see all that you have is everything that I need. Help me to begin to view my situation as beautiful no matter how broken it may seem. Help me to dig into all the secret places of my mind and my heart as I read this book. I want you to be able to fill all of me with who you are. Even the secret places that I have tried to hide from you. Fill me with your love, freedom, and life as I walk through this brokenness into your beauty.

In Jesus' name, amen.

WORD

There are people all throughout the Bible that were completely shattered, and God used them to bring about the greatest glory for His kingdom. He is all about capturing His lost and broken kids and helping them to see the beauty in it all. Joseph was rejected by his family, sold into slavery and forced into a life not his own. Daniel, a young teen, was thrown into the lion's den. Saul/Paul was living a life as a murderer and killing Christians. Noah was rejected by many for believing in the vision that God had placed on his heart. David was thrown into the shepherd's field as a young boy while his brothers lived a life of favor with their dad. Jesus on the cross, bloody, and broken had all His life drained from Him. This list only consists of a few of God's wounded but victorious warriors.

In each one of these situations, there is beauty found in their brokenness. Joseph ends up in a house that brings provisions to the ones who abandoned him. Daniel receives power to sustain life in the den. Saul/Paul endures a transformation that creates a desire to present the Gospel to a nation. Noah receives life and promise for all future humanity. David receives authority to lead a nation. Jesus receives resurrection and salvation for all to live for eternity. God knew that we would experience a broken life. He wanted us to see through His word that He would bring beauty out of it all.

WORSHIP

Listen to "Defender" by Upper Room. This song is about God being your defender. The one who saved you and loves you. Listen as you think only about the love God has for you even in your dark moments.

LINK LEVERAGE TOOL

AWARENESS
- Write three words that stood out to you while reading this chapter.

ASK
- Ask yourself what did these words speak to you?

GOAL
- Write down one goal that will help you to grow this week.

CHANGE
- What change can you make to acheive your goal?

SERVE
- Who did I serve this week and how did it make me feel?

ILLUMINATION

Use this journal to write three valuable nuggets that you learned in this chapter and how you have won in life because of them. Then write three things you are thankful for. Look for the light in your darkness.

_____
_____
_____
_____
_____
_____
_____
_____
_____
_____
_____
_____
_____
_____
_____
_____
_____
_____
_____
_____
_____
_____
_____

1 Corinthians 13:4-8 (NIV)
"Love is patient, love is kind. It does not envy; it does not boast; it is not proud. It does not dishonor others; it is not self-seeking, it is not easily angered, it keeps no record of wrongs. It does not delight in evil but rejoices with the truth. It always protects, always trust, always hopes always perseveres. Love never fails."

Use this page to draw what is on your mind, write out scriptures that stand out or quotes that speak to you.

STEP 2
RECALL THE MOMENTS

"Don't just recall the storm, recall the beauty of color that comes from the storm."

AFRESH

That moment when you realize it's over. When you realize they are gone. When you realize the pain is real. When you hear the diagnosis. When your baby is born. On your wedding day—do you remember any of these moments? We all have a "that moment" from our journey called life. That moment we will never forget, the moment that is etched in our mind forever. It can be good or bad, but it is a moment that is unforgettable.

We have heard the saying all our lives, "Make every moment count." When we realize every moment leads to the full story of our lives, we begin to see every moment as a piece worthy of being recalled. We must make every moment count, even the ones that have brought about brokenness in our lives. When we see that there is a bigger purpose for every one of our stories it creates opportunities and desires to recall them all.

Recalling moments is something we all do. It may be in the quietness of our hearts, rooms, and lives or out in the open for all to see and hear. The recall of the moments, both good and bad, are inevitable. As you are reading this, you may be saying "Recall? WHAT? I don't want to recall or remember any of my moments that have crushed me. I want just to move on like it never happened, and just think about the happy moments. If I don't think about it, won't it just go away?" Wrong!

So many times, in the weakness of our brokenness, we want to discount, hide or suppress our true feelings instead of bringing out the truth of our emotions. We are told by many to suck it up, move on, or it will only hurt for a little while, or there will be a new normal. Then when the pain continues to pour in, we feel like we are weird, abnormal or misunderstood. This feeling then creates isolation. It becomes a habit to withdrawal and disguise our pain. The isolation in return hides us in the mangled mess of our today and yesterday.

You cannot just move on in your brokenness, you need to talk about it with others. It is not only a moment for you to recall so that you can remove it from the painful category to the beautiful category, it is also moved to a place of illumination so that others can see that they are not walking their similar journey alone.

When we are in a time where our life feels fractured, the focus tends to be on the one who is fractured. We think that life is all about us and that there is nothing or no one else in the world that could understand or obtain anything from "the moment." If I share, I will seem weak and weird. The thoughts arise that no one could understand the depth of our pain. The thought that our story is not as bad as the one dealing with the death of a spouse, cancer or a problem that we view as being way bigger than our painful moment, silences us.

God cares about all our pain and brokenness and wants to take what the devil means for bad and turn it into something powerful for His glory. So, do not minimize your pain. It is real, and it will eat you alive from the inside out if you do not find someone to talk to. Someone that will listen to what you are going through and help you walk through the journey of healing. This person may be an accountability partner, counselor, life coach, pastor or your link partner. It is imperative to recall and put your pain out there, so you can deal with it. Allow others to be a part of your journey. Isolation is the avenue to defeat, destruction and eventually death.

I recall the first time I shared my story. It was with a pastor at ITOWN church in Fishers, Indiana. I called the church in one of my darkest moments and asked to speak with someone because I felt like I had no hope or life left in me. I was on my way to the hospital to get help if I didn't feel better quick. I was so overcome with the darkness of my emotions and my sin at that moment. As I began to share my story with the pastor, she just listened to me. I shared with this woman the deepest parts of my wounds, insecurities, and failures. I immediately began to feel healing come from those sore places. It was like an ointment put on an open wound that had become infected. There was immediate relief.

Sometimes we need to get things off our chest because the secrets that we keep about our true feelings and sin are a doorway for the enemy to have control of our hearts. It creates an opportunity for him to put weights and chains on us that will hold us back from our destiny and dreams.

She eventually, when I took a breath, prayed for me and used the Word to encourage me, which created an opportunity for more freedom to come into my life. Her response to me was full of grace, tenderness, and love. The grace, tenderness, and love that she displayed opened the door for me to then be confident to share with my closest friends and family. Up to this point, no one knew about the sin, anger towards God, thoughts of unworthiness, lies or pain of what I had been walking in. Each time I shared I felt such a release. Sharing the recall of brokenness would lighten the weight of my story and then I could see the illumination in the story instead of the darkness. There is healing in recalling your moment.

How do I Begin the Recall Process?

First, pray that God will help you to recall all moments that have affected or infected your life. Pray that He will help you to have the confidence to share and the wisdom to understand the beauty of your brokenness.
Here is a prayer to pray if you are stuck on what to say:

Jesus, I know that you had to recall your moments of brokenness for life to come to all. If you didn't recall your story for me, where would I be today? I know it was not easy, but you saw the beauty in the whole moment. You say in your word that the same power that is in you, lives in me. Help me to understand this power as I prepare to share my moments—all of them. Help me to see the victory in all the moments of my life. In Jesus' name, amen.

Second, get off the self-pity roller coaster. The pity roller coaster is not a ride you want to be on or that anyone will get on with you. JUMP OFF as fast as you can. When telling your story, it is not so that you can gain pity and have people join your party. It is so that you can bring to light the darkness inside of your heart and then it can be drowned out by the light of Christ.

The enemy wants nothing more than to get you stuck in the darkness of self-pity. In that place, you get trapped on the continuous high and low dips of emotions. Remember, recalling your story is to bring the pain to the surface and dispose of it.

Dispose of it to the light of what Christ brings from it. Darkness can never dwell in the light or illumination.

Third, you have found your missing link: your link partner who is helping you walk through this process. So, open up and begin to share the deepest wounds and secrets you are housing in your heart now. Use the resource Figure 1:1 to write down the moments of your life that have caused darkness and death that you need to share. Every situation we walk through is a situation of salvation for someone.

When you are thinking about your recall moments and how to present them, do not get stuck on the idea of being broken. Recall what happened first. Think about the story and how you realize it was a moment of brokenness. Then put some recognition to the way it made you feel. Did you feel dirty, sad, mad, hurt, unworthy? Did you recognize the emotion of it all? As Christians, we try to wear a mask and hide the emotion in our brokenness. It is real, and we need to expose it to our recall. Anything hidden in the dark will eventually present to the light. It will be brought to the light by our doing, a situation we get caught doing or God. Which way would you prefer to be exposed?

Fourth, focus on what you learned in the middle of it all. There is wisdom you can gain in all situations. When the story is playing out, the lessons can be hard to see. It is in the hard-to-see moments that the pretending begins to be our norm. God is forever trying to bring us to a growth point. The growth point is a point that will lead you and others closer to the cross. Ask your link partner to help you if you are having trouble viewing your situation as a time of growth. People on the outside can see things that we drown out on the inside. If you open yourself up, be willing to listen to what they say.

Finally, ask yourself at this moment what can you use to help someone else. Once you see the beauty in your story, the light of God will bring people to you that can be helped by that beauty. When you see something beautiful, it is hard to take your eyes off it. Attractive is how you will be viewed by those that are hurting. When the light of Christ is what is beaming out of you, this is attractive.

I was at work one day while walking down the journey of recalling my moments. In this piece of my journey, a lady approached my cubicle and said, "I need to ask you something. Why are you so different? You are always happy, and you have this 'thing' about you that I don't understand." It was the awareness of the beauty through the recall that caused me to start acting differently. The recognition helped me to become attractive again. I am not talking about an outward beauty but an inward and beyond-me beauty. She then gave me the opportunity to share my story with her, and I invited her to church. That week she and her entire family came. Change can happen for others when you recall your moments. However, do not tell your story to get a response from the listener. Tell it to get a response from your heart.

Figure1:1

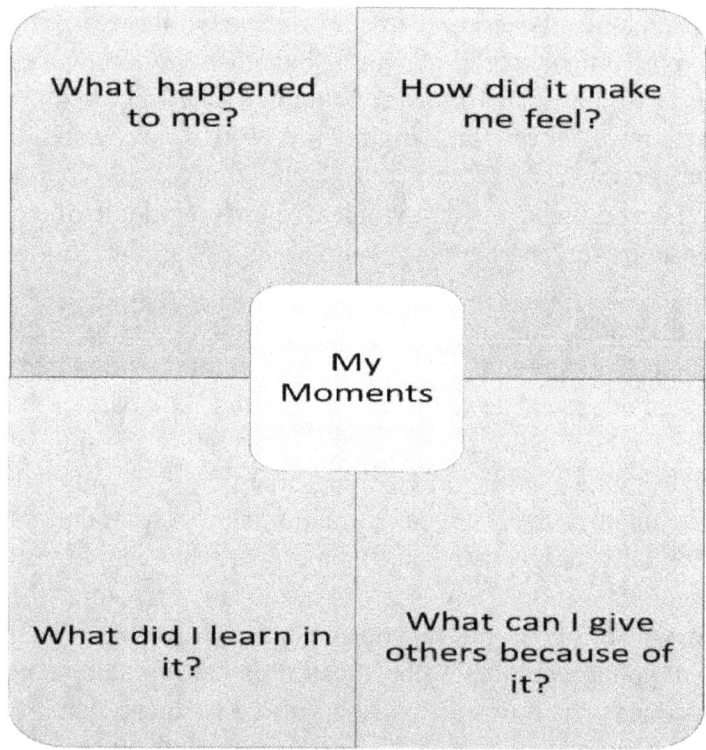

Reasons We Hide from the Recall

There are reasons we try to hide from the recall. One of those reasons might be the rejection that may come if we share our story. Is your recall one filled with lust, abandonment, insecurity, faithlessness, and/or hopelessness? You may think, who can love a broken piece of work like me? This myth needs to be busted, and the only way to do that is to recall your story with your link partner and watch how they respond with love and acceptance.

Another reason we hide from our recall is we may feel like a failure. This may be because of the mistakes we have made that are tied to our pain place. There are a lot of mistakes that can be a part of the darkness we allow in our lives. Mistakes of pride, causing pain to others, choices and walking away from our purpose. Just remember what good ole' Walt Disney said, "Everyone falls down. Getting up is how you learn to walk." We all have fallen and failed at some point in our lives, and it is in that moment that we find success also. Don't just see the storm, see the beauty of color that comes from that storm.

We also think we can "Fake it until you make it. This is something I heard so many times during my process of being beautifully broken. I heard it from others and from my own distorted thinking. So, I thought if I hid from the recall and just faked it, I would forget it. I thought this way of thinking would allow me to move on. However, I don't see anything in scripture to back this up. There will not be any victory that comes when you fake the recall or fake the joy. You must walk through the process of recall so that you can then see the victory that comes from the whole story not just see the moment. If you fake it, you are just avoiding the brokenness and the beauty. Faking it will cause you to stay stuck on a merry-go-round that is full of lack of trust, fear, and insecurity.

Fear of being hurt again is a very popular reason we avoid the recall. We close ourselves down as a protection device. If we recall and share our story, we then become vulnerable, which will open us up to possible hurt. Hurt is what put me in this spot of brokenness in the first place. Why would I want to open the door to pain for myself again? With this fear, we need to understand what it says in 2 Timothy 1:7 (KJV) *"For God hath not given us a spirit of fear; but of power, and of love, and of a sound mind."* God will take the fear away if you call on Him. Fear is always a sign of false evidence that is presenting itself in a realistic manner. The reality is it that this is a big fat lie. Drown out the fake, the false and the fear with the truth of God and watch what happens in your situation.

Begin to view your recall as a stepping-stone to the promises of your tomorrow. In your brokenness, failure is inevitable if we try to do it alone. We are like a tent without pegs in a storm.
Alone the tent will fly away from its original placement. When the pegs are securing the tent, even in the storm, it will not be moved from its original place. Therefore, we recall our story with and for others, so we can remain in the promise that God takes the good, bad and ugly, and shines through them.

REALITY RECALL

By Kevin Massey

In February 2010 I had just turned 16-years-old when I received the diagnosis of an inoperable brain tumor. I was a three-sport varsity athlete in high school, with high hopes to attend the University of Kentucky, the college of my dreams. The dream included playing basketball for them.

Those dreams all came to a screeching halt when my family got the news that I would only live for 24 -48 hours. My family dwelled in an overwhelming sense of loss and sadness. In the middle of this hopelessness, God had a bigger, beautiful plan. He would heal me. I lived! I am a walking miracle, which doctors have declared as part of my medical journey.

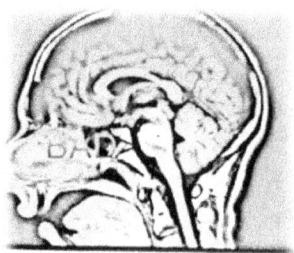 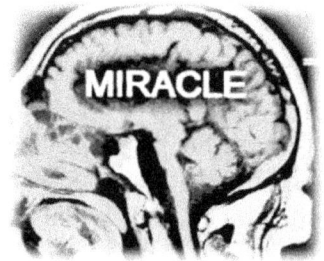

Figure 1:2

These are the before and after scans performed by the doctors. They labeled them as bad and miracle.

I was paralyzed on my right side, so to play basketball for UK was no longer a possibility. When I woke up out of a coma, I began to realize that I was broken both physically and emotionally. I initially held these thoughts inside but soon realized that others needed to hear my story of hope and healing. I began to recall the story and share it with others.

Recalling this moment of loss caused me to see the gain for others and myself. In this recall, it brought a significant amount of healing to my own life. I am now a graduate of the University of Kentucky, with a degree in communications. I was part of the basketball team as a student manager. My recall helped me to move forward and chase new dreams.

It is evident that if I did not recall and share my story with the world, it could have placed me in a cell of fear. I may have spent the rest of my life trying to break out of that cell without the key to the recall. This fear could have caused me to just sit around and wait to die.

The doctors told my family that I would not talk, eat, walk or live a productive life ever again. I shut them down, and I am still proving them all wrong today. I continue moving forward not just for myself but also for others. Do the same: recall and share your brokenness, your moment, your story— you never know who's waiting for the recall to bring them hope for their future.

ESPN did a story on Kevin during the final four of 2015. If you want to view the video, go to the Beautifully Broken Facebook page facebook.com/Cheri-Gable-344699785938586 and go to the videos section. Also, to book Kevin Massey for a speaking engagement contact Unite Life Coaching at 317-989-0022 or Unitelifecoaching@gmail.com.

MEDITATION MOMENTS

STILL MOMENT

Set a timer for two minutes and rest in God as you prepare to recall your story. At this moment, do not write, sing or dance. It is time to be still, breathe in God, and breathe out your pain.

PRAYER

God,

Help me to recall my story so that I can begin to see the victories and strength that are wrapped up in it. Help me to be illuminated by you so that I can spread goodness and truth to the world.

In Jesus' name, amen.

WORD

There is a recall displayed in every word from the front to the back of the Holy Bible. In John 1:1(NIV) it states that *"In the beginning was the Word, the Word was with God, and the Word was God."* The Bible is a display of what a recall of your story would be. If Jesus would not have recalled His broken moments for us to see, how would we be able to see the great victory that can come through our brokenness? What if he just shared all the good moments? Would it be possible for humanity to see the greatness that can come from our broken moments in life? Jesus had the ultimate broken moments on his way to the cross, as he had the crown of thorns placed on his head, as he hung on the cross, as he was put in a cave and had a stone rolled in front of it. His story is one of death, darkness, defeat and destruction. However, as you read the recall, you see that it was those moments that led to the greatest victory of Jesus' life: HIS RESURRECTION.

No matter how dark your moment may be now, there is a resurrection coming. Recall your moment with someone the way Jesus did with us and enjoy the resurrection you find in it.

WORSHIP

John 4:24 (NIV) *"God is spirit, and those who worship him must worship him in spirit and in truth."*

Listen to the song "Rez Power" by Israel and New Breed. This is a song on the resurrection of Christ, and it will allow your spirit to come back to life.

LINK LEVERAGE TOOL

AWARENESS
- Write three words that stood out to you while reading this chapter.

ASK
- Ask yourself what did these words speak to you?

GOAL
- Write down one goal that will help you to grow this week.

CHANGE
- What change can you make to acheive your goal?

SERVE
- Who did I serve this week and how did it make me feel?

ILLUMINATION

Use this journal to write three valuable nuggets that you learned in this chapter and how you have won in life because of them. Then write three things you are thankful for. Look for the light in your darkness.

_____
_____
_____
_____
_____
_____
_____
_____
_____
_____
_____
_____
_____
_____
_____
_____
_____
_____
_____
_____
_____
_____
_____
_____
_____
_____

Sometimes miracles show up in the smallest forms, don't overlook them.

Use this page to draw what is on your mind, write out scriptures that stand out or quotes that speak to you.

STEP 3
REVIVE THE HEART

Tell your heart to beat again! In your impossible thinking, God can bring the possibility to life.

AFRESH

Love. Love is a word used by many poets, musical artists, ancient philosophers and God. In times of brokenness, it is hard to feel the love for yourself, the love that others are giving, or possibly even the love of God. In your brokenness, your heart may stop beating, and you may quit breathing. It may feel like the wind was knocked out of you. In this step, you must tell your heart to beat again. Tell it to beat for yourself, to beat for God and to beat for others.

The heart is a representation of love and life, but if your heart has died, can you love? The heart and lungs work hand in hand to supply oxygen to the cells of the body. When the heart stops beating it affects all other functions. You can't walk, talk, eat, see, hear or touch. Everything begins to shut down and goes blank or black. Therefore, we need our hearts to beat again. We need to see again, think again, feel again, begin to walk again, but most importantly our lives need to be illuminated again with the love of God.

Defib is short for a defibrillator, a device used to shock the heart to make it beat normal again. During brokenness what you see above all else is the destruction of your past and present but no hope for the future. Proverbs 13:12 (NIV) states, *"Hope deferred makes the heart sick, but a dream fulfilled is a tree of life."* Our hearts become sick with the lies that we are not worthy of love and that there is no hope for us.

What flows from the heart during these times? The Bible states in Luke 6:45 (NIV) *"A good man brings good things out of the good stored up in his heart, and an evil man brings evil things out of the evil stored up in his heart. The mouth speaks what the heart is full of."* Words flow from our heart and create life or death. Is there life flowing from your lips? What are you speaking today about God, yourself and others? Take time to evaluate this by using Figure 2:1

Figure 2:1: *In this exercise list four things you said about God today. Then under the "yourself" graph, list four things you said about yourself today. Next, list four people you encountered today and write three things you spoke to them or about them, good or bad. It only helps you if you are honest in this exercise. See the example below.*

God (EXAMPLE)

Not Available	Good	Loving	Kind

Yourself (EXAMPLE)

Ugly	Fat	Successful	Broken

Others (EXAMPLE)

Example: Mom	Boss	The person at the grocery	Pastor
Loving	Needy	Stupid	Helpful

When this exercise is walked out—if you're honest with yourself—it will give you a clear picture of what state your heart is in and if your allegiance is with love or hate. I know hate is a strong word. In the state of pain and darkness, we often align with hate. Hate is defined as intense or passionate dislike.

In those moments that we feel like we have failed to the point of no return, love is thrown aside, and hate is ignited. Hate brings death and is not a fruit of the spirit. Hate destroys the heart and causes death to be presented to everyone you encounter.

I have never seen a dead person, but in movies, you see it all the time. My dad is a big action, killing movie, kind of guy. If I watch movies with him, it is all about the death and gore. It's not my choice, but I love my dad enough to watch them with him on occasion. Whenever the death of someone happens, I will turn my head, cover my face and sometimes scream. The covering is what happens when we become the walking dead because of hate and hurt. People will cover themselves or run from us because they do not want to be a part of the death, we are bringing to them.

Love is a beautiful flow that comes from a heart that is beating at the right pace. An accurate heartbeat creates a steady flow of oxygen that will cause you to breathe. Breathing goodness on people as well as yourself, are signs that the heart is in rhythm with the creator. How can the flow of love and life be created?

By Loving God

First, you must create a heart full of love for God again. In the pain of our past and present, we begin to blame God. We may ask God, "Why?" Why did he allow the death of our loved one? Why did he allow the divorce? Why me? Why this? Why now? Why then? The big WHY GOD WHY drives us to a place of insanity and directly into a relationship with the enemy. Doubt is a part of everyone's faith journey at one point or another—doubt about their faith, God, Bible or Christianity in general. Doubt is part of the human condition and is in the Bible in many stories such as Thomas, Gideon, and Moses—just to name a few. It is one of the key factors to our heart not beating and flowing with a love for God.

Let's look at a story in Judges 6 (NIV) where you can see Gideon doubting God. An angel of the Lord comes to Gideon in verse 12 and says, *"The Lord is with you, mighty warrior!"* Gideon could not believe what was being spoken. He had allowed his situation to cause his heart to stop beating and believing in God. Gideon says in verse 13, *"If the Lord is with us, WHY has all of this happened to us?* This is the standard question we all ask: "Why?"

The Midianites had oppressed and impoverished the Israelites in a way that brought great brokenness. The brokenness caused the Israelites to prepare a shelter for themselves in the mountain clefts, caves and strongholds. How many times do we hide in caves and walk into strongholds when we are doubting and broken? Gideon was the one God was calling to help them break free from the doubt and fear that the Midianites had created. However, Gideon was questioning if this was God. He said in Judges 6:13 (NIV), *"... but if the Lord is with us, why has all this happened to us? Where are all His wonders that our ancestors told us about when they said, 'Did not the Lord bring us up out of Egypt?' But now the Lord has abandoned us and given us into the hand of Midian (the enemy)."*

How many times do we sound like Gideon when we are in our situations of brokenness? We think God has abandoned us. I know that this is how I felt in my brokenness. I felt like I had failed God and His punishment to me was abandonment. This is a lie from the enemy used to get us to resist the unconditional love that flows from Gods heart. His heart beats with love for us in all situations. God says to Gideon, *"Go in the strength you have and save Israel out of the Midian's hands."* Then Gideon says, *"BUT..."* Many times, in your hurt and pain God calls you to do something and you say, "but God."

God is so in love with you, and He believes in you always. Just ask God to show you how much He loves you and then begin to look at the ways He will display His love to you. Gideon said, *"God can you squash my doubt and fear by displaying yourself to me in a real way?"* Gideon was paralyzed with fear and doubt. This doubt left him feeling uncertain and unworthy. The whole time he is walking in his negative emotions, he is delaying his impact on the people God had assigned him to help. He laid out some specific ways that God could show him he was real in this situation, and God showed up and showed off for Gideon. He will do the same for you—for us! In your impossible thinking, God can bring the possibility to life.

The story of Gideon reminds me of a personal situation while drafting this book. I am called by God to author this book and to have a Beautifully Broken conference all over the world. These two ministries are going to help a multitude of broken individuals that have been impoverished by the enemy. It took me what seemed like forever to complete the writing. When I finished the writing process, I was filled with an enthusiastic sense of accomplishment and was very encouraged. *God really used me*, I thought. I could not believe that He really could use me to do something so big for His Kingdom. Next, all I needed to do was send it to the editor, make corrections and get it published. It seemed like my heart was paralyzed and I could not breathe enough to complete the task.

One Saturday morning I was at a friend's house to help her prepare for her son's graduation party. I woke up and began to do a devotion. I felt God drawing me downstairs. When I got downstairs my friend was sitting in the living room reading a devotion and said to me, "God is encouraging me to read this to you." She read a devotion to me about doing good things, but they are not the God things. She stated that they were not what He had called me to do in this season, and they are delaying me. She began to cry and tell me that I had lost my focus. I love friends/link partners that are not afraid to be honest. I began to feel something come to the surface of my heart. It was a revelation of the fear of failure that I did not realize I had allowed to enter until that moment. I had begun to view myself in the eyes of failure instead of the eyes of God's love. My heart had stopped beating for the dreams and vision that God for my life.

I would like to say the story ended there and I completed the book right away and got it published, but I still sat on an incomplete book. This is when my link partner, Linda Orange, came alongside me during a 21-day fast and said, "we are getting this book done." She edited it for me in a matter of 3 days and then held me accountable until it was complete and in the publisher's hands. God has a fantastic way of helping you to push through your delays. He also has a certain setup of people ready to pull the defib machine out, place the paddles on your chest and create a regular heartbeat again. Don't reject the godsends that God delivers into your life during specific seasons.

I had come to realize that I was frozen by the idea of what if I failed people and God again? Could God use me when I failed Him so hard the last time, He called me to something so big? I realized doubt in God's love for me had stopped me in the purposeful path that God had set me on, again. My friend instructed me that I had to view my situation and brokenness differently. I had to view it all as prep for my now and my future in God. I had to begin to believe that God loved me and believed in me enough to give me this assignment and He would be the victory in it. Victory belongs to Jesus. Victory comes to God and to us when we recognize His love for us, and the power wrapped in His love.

John 3:16 tells us of this great love. A love that is willing to sacrifice it all, a love that is willing to put on a public display so that we can see his radical love, along with others. I had to realize that God always loves us, and nothing comes to us unless it goes through Him first. God's love for me is fierce and unrelenting. He didn't stop on me; I am the one that stopped my pursuit of Him.

Some questions may never be answered here on earth but trust in the fact that Jesus is beyond in love with you! He loves you so much that He was willing to go through some brutal things for your eternal salvation. You may have to walk through some tough situations, but remember that Jesus overcame, and He will help you to overcome. Also, remember that every situation that you go through is all about directing people to faith and eternity the same way Jesus did with you. When you keep an eternity perspective, you keep a Jesus perspective.

I know that this is hard to do amid pain. I struggled with this myself. At one point in my journey, I was screaming at God saying, "WHY? WHY?" But this only led me to confusion and more tragedy. Only when I started seeing my situations as a blessing and beautifully broken did things change. Allow your heart to beat again with the understanding of God's passionate love for you.
You are HIS!

By Loving Myself

Another way to get your heart to respond to the flow again is to begin to love yourself again. Many times, we allow our brokenness and failure to define us. Once it defines you, you begin to live out the failure repeatedly. You see yourself as nothing but a broken, fragmented mess on the floor of life. You see yourself as not being useful or worthy. What you need to understand is that you can only love yourself when you understand who you are and whose you are. So, who are you? Where can your identity be found? Is it found in a bunch of shattered pieces? Is your identity found in failure or is it found in faith?

If you were to look in a mirror right now what would you see? Let's do this: Get a mirror out and look directly at yourself. Write the words that come to mind in the mirror below:

Many times, you will define yourself by who you know, which leads you to be a people-pleaser. You begin running around trying to please the world, never feeling the sense of contentment in who you were created to be. When you find your identity in this place, you could fall into the hands of wrong relationships. This pattern will lead you to a destiny of destructive patterns and continuously wanting to be chosen by others when you have already been picked by God. He chose you! You were handpicked and created by Him.

Another way we define ourselves is by what we do. This definition causes our worth and identity to be tied to our achievements. The side effect of this is when we fail, it is the end of the world. We have a challenging time seeing past our failure.

Incorrect identity can also be found in the way we identify ourselves by our appearance. This identity leads to a desire to be the prettiest at any cost. The side effect of this type of identity is vanity and narcissism—making everything about us and how we look. Our focus becomes distorted, self-centered, and full of selfish ambitions and desires.

Now let's compare this to how you see yourself when you look in the mirror of the Word. Look up these scriptures and write the words that define who it says you are.

John 1:12 _____
Ephesians 1:5_____
Romans 15:7 _____
Colossians 2:9-10_____
Corinthians 6:17_____
Romans 6:6 _____
Jeremiah 1:5_____
1 Corinthians 12:27 _____
1 Peter 2:9 _____

You are described in the Word as being a child of God, a chosen one, royalty, holy, God's special possession, set apart, appointed, new creation—this list goes on and on. Stick this page in a place where you can view it daily. Begin to confess your identity in Christ. Your confession is who you become. Confess defeat and you will feel defeated. Confess life and feel life. Confess love and be love. Speak blessings over your identity daily so that you can walk in the understanding and blessing of who you were created to be.

By Loving Others

Once you understand Christ's love for you and you understand how to love yourself, then you will understand that Christ is the greatest example of how to love others again. In our brokenness, it is possible to lose faith in people. Our hearts become cold and we tend to shut off our emotions and our compassion for people in general. God sent His son even when we were in sin. He so loved the world that He was willing to die for it.

When it comes to loving others, how can we follow the example of Christ? He first showed His display of love for the world while here on this Earth by finding His way into their story. Think about the people that He displayed love to as he healed, brought back to life, fed and died to save. He had to know what the need was before He could meet the need. Begin to put yourself out there again to hear the stories of others. You will never know how your journey intertwines with others if you don't begin to care about others again.

Secondly, He served them. Matthew 20:28 (NIV) states: *"Just as the Son of Man did not come to be served, but to serve, and to give his life as a ransom for many."* This is the way that we can begin to love others. We serve them, and in serving them, we gain their trust, which gives birth to relationships. In relationships, you begin to develop a love for people. Loving others is a mandate from Christ. If we do not love, we are said to be *"nothing but a resounding gong"* according to 1 Corinthians 13:1. How annoying is that sound? It is a like whistle that is continually blown or a horn that is being honked continuously for no reason. These sounds are annoying and create anger and frustration in people. We want to love others and create a wonderful sound of Christ that draws others to the cross.

But What is true love anyway?

In general, the question most commonly asked when talking about love with the brokenhearted is: "What is true love anyway?" The answer to this question is found in 1 Corinthians 13:4-7. Read the scripture and then write a list out of what it says true love is.

_____   _____   _____

_____   _____   _____

_____   _____

What does it say true love is not or does not do in that same scripture?

_____   _____   _____

_____   _____   _____

_____

True love is patient, kind, keeps no record of wrongs, rejoices in truth, always protects, always trust, always hopes, and always perseveres. It is not envious, boastful, proud, dishonorable, self-seeking, easily angered, and it does not delight in evil. This scripture can be used to gain a deep understanding of how to align with love and tell your heart to beat again. You align by committing to continuously evaluating your love for God, yourself, and others. Are you displaying everything that love is said to be?

REALITY RECALL

By Joel Pollock

Alone. Lost. Helpless. Broken. Yes, "broken." That probably described best how I was feeling. Maybe even "beyond broken." I was staring at a divorce. Not just a divorce, but a second divorce (unfortunately, I'd done this once before). I was also coming to grips with the fact that I had an addiction to alcohol that had taken over my life. And I still had the same insecurities of failure, not being good enough, rejection, etc., that I had been dealing with for the past twenty years of my life. So yes, "broken" was indeed a word I felt comfortable with, or as comfortable as you can be with a word like broken. I had labeled myself "broken beyond repair." The view of my world was this:

Every time I stepped out of my house, I had to wear a jacket, or armor of sorts. On this jacket, there was a "D" on one sleeve, which stood for Divorce. On the other sleeve, there was an "A" for Alcoholic. And in the middle of my chest, there was a great big "F" for Failure. It didn't matter where I went—to the store, to the gas station, to work— and it didn't matter whether you knew me or not. One thing was certain in my mind: You looked at me as if I was one of the most pitiful things you had ever laid your eyes upon. You didn't have to say a word to me (because the sight of me may make you sick), but I decided for you how you felt about me. And I decided that you looked at me and thought I was broken.

But therein lies the beauty of things that are broken. Broken doesn't have to mean ruined. It doesn't have to mean finished. Broken can be overcome by things such as time, healing, support, repair, etc.—and those were all things I needed. But how? My life had become so full of voids throughout the last twenty years. These voids led to insecurities, which led to poor life choices, which led me to lose my wife (and essentially a really good friend in alcohol), which led to overwhelming feelings of emptiness, loneliness, and brokenness. How was I to find some way to fill these voids and to start healing, so I did not have to stay broken? I stared beyond the divorce, beyond the addiction, beyond the insecurities, beyond the brokenness, right into nothing. I literally stared out into the space surrounding me with no thoughts or emotions, until I finally threw out these words:

"God, I know this is not the way my life is supposed to go. I've lost my way. I know I have turned away from you for too long now. God, would you please just help me to make things right in my life. I don't know what I'm doing anymore. I just want help."

I felt comfortable asking God for help, despite the fact at that point in my life, I had been away from God for too long. I grew up as the son of a pastor. When I was a child, I loved going to church and helping my dad during the services whenever I was able. But as I went off to college and into adulthood, I lost my way. I allowed the world to consume me. But this cry out to God was my way of turning back to Him and letting Him know I realized the error of my ways.

Shortly after this cry out for help, a good friend invited me to his church. I started attending this church weekly. It was the most life-giving, Spirit filled place I had ever been. This was where I was going to continue growing closer to God in order to move beyond the wounds, beyond the loneliness, beyond the brokenness.

I started getting involved in the church's small groups as a way to connect with people throughout the week and as a way to develop lasting relationships. I started serving on a team at church— the Kids Team because I've always had a passion for helping children. I started reading my Bible more often. I prayed daily. I pulled myself away from chasing after things of this world and put my focus on God and my relationship with Him.

Over the next year, I found myself never wanting to miss a weekend at church. I attended services every week. I continued to attend small groups and eventually I even helped lead some. I not only served more often in the kid's room, but I also became one of the leaders on the Kids Team. I attended prayer services regularly. I even went on a mission trip! I still had time to do things I always enjoyed doing such as going to the gym, watching football and basketball, hanging out with friends, watching movies, and relaxing. The difference was, I knew where God stood in my life. He was no longer a way for me to ask for help from time to time—He was my priority. By putting God first and letting everything else fall into place, I started to fill all the voids in my life with positive things, things I enjoyed doing and doing with passion.

Nearly two years have passed since the moment I was staring at complete brokenness. I still have the memories of how I felt during that time. But time has passed, support was given, and the healing has come. I have asked God for forgiveness for the wrong I have done, and by His grace, I know I am forgiven. I have asked God to allow me to forgive those who have hurt me in the past so that I am not burdened by feelings of anger, resentment, and jealousy. I ask God daily to allow me to follow his will for my life, and I grow closer to him every day. I have asked God to allow me to replace the wrong things I had in my life with the right things. And at this moment in life, I can honestly say I am filled with the love, joy, and peace that He so dearly wants for each of us. I would never ask that the experiences I went through be taken from me or erased from my mind. If I could do it all over again, I wouldn't ask for anything to change. The wounds and scars I have from those experiences are a testament to how far I've come, and how far God has brought me. I can live to tell my story.

MEDITATION MOMENTS

STILL MOMENTS
Set a timer for three minutes and rest in God as you meditate on Christ's love for you and your love for yourself and others.

PRAYER
God,

Thank you so much for allowing your Spirit to ignite my heart again and cause it to beat with your love. I always want to love big and surround myself with the same kind of love that you showed me on the cross. I love you so much, and I know that even in my failure, doubt, and fears you continuously love me. In Jesus' name, amen

WORD
In the word, Christ used the defib of love to bring many back to life. One story that captures my heart for this chapter is the one of Lazarus. He was one of Jesus' closest friends. Lazarus was in allegiance with Christ's love. Jesus had information brought to him that Lazarus had died. He did not go to him right away, but when he went, he saw the people weeping. It says in John 11:33 (NIV) that he was deeply moved by this display of love that Lazarus' sisters and the community had for this man. Then Jesus said to them, *"Where is he laid?"* They took Jesus to the spot and scripture says, *"Jesus wept."* Out of the mouths of some of the people that were there flowed these words, *"See how he loved him!"* There is

an explanation point at the end of that scripture to bring to light the intensity of love that Jesus had for Lazarus. His love eventually calls Lazarus from the grave and creates in him life again. When you have a heart that beats with the love of Christ, that love will always flow back to you and bring life to your dead situations.

WORSHIP

During your worship time listen to "Tremble" by Mosaic. It is a song about calling on the name of Jesus. When you call on this name it will cause your lungs to sing, your heart to beat and the enemy of fear to be silenced.

LINK LEVERAGE TOOL

AWARENESS
- Write three words that stood out to you while reading this chapter.

ASK
- Ask yourself what did these words speak to you?

GOAL
- Write down one goal that will help you to grow this week.

CHANGE
- What change can you make to acheive your goal?

SERVE
- Who did I serve this week and how did it make me feel?

ILLUMINATION

Use this journal to write three valuable nuggets that you learned in this chapter and how you have won in life because of them. Then write three things you are thankful for. Look for the light in your darkness.

_____
_____
_____
_____
_____
_____
_____
_____
_____
_____
_____
_____
_____
_____
_____
_____
_____
_____
_____
_____
_____
_____
_____
_____
_____
_____
_____

Colossians 3:14-17 (NIV) "And above all these put-on love which binds it all together in perfect harmony. And let the peace of Christ rule in your hearts, to which indeed you were called in one body. And be thankful."

Use this page to draw what is on your mind, write out scriptures that stand out or quotes that speak to you.

STEP 4
RECEIVE THE FOUNTAINS OF GRACE

You can't have sufficient grace if you do not tap into the fountain that grace dwells within.

AFRESH

Out of Jesus' mouth flowed these words in 2 Corinthians 12:9 (NIV) *"My grace is sufficient for you, for my power is made perfect in weakness."* Jesus' power being perfect depends on me being weak. Have you ever considered weakness as a sign of someone that was powerless and broken? Me too, on many occasions, until Jesus had me read and reread this scripture. He said in 2 Corinthians 12:9, *"His power is put on display when I am weak."*

See it like this: If I tapped myself into electricity by putting my finger in an outlet, what do I get? A jolt of electricity. If I am tapped into a flow of water what do I get? Water. If my veins are tapped into an IV, I get whatever is in the IV bag. What are you tapped into and what are you receiving? The opposite of grace is unforgiveness and judgment. The longing of our heart should be to tap into the fountains of grace that God gives. You can't have sufficient grace if you don't tap into the one that fountains of grace dwell in.

Fountains of Grace produces:

Look up these scriptures to see what you get with grace:
Acts 6:8 _____
Acts 6:8 _____
Acts 6:9 _____
Acts 14:3 _____
Acts 15:11 _____
Acts 20:32 _____
Acts 20:32 _____
Hebrews 13:9 _____

It has been said by many, time and time again, that grace is talked about in the church too much. If grace produces all of this, then how can it be talked about too much? Understanding grace will draw you to power and freedom. Grace will produce growth, miracles, signs, wonders, salvation, testimony, inheritance, and strengthened hearts, just to name a few. In the New Testament grace is mentioned over 150 times. In our brokenness we need to realize that Jesus is the fountain of grace that never runs dry.

It is in this grace that you will find the power to surrender all and move into your purpose continuously. Have you ever felt like you were stuck on the merry-go-round of doubt, insecurity, and fear? —like you did not know how to jump off, but you were continuously feeling dizzy, disoriented and sick? The only way to have the courage to jump off is to understand and to tap into the fountain of the grace. Drench yourself in this fountain and watch how powerful you will become for heaven's purpose, not your own.

Read Acts 9. Did you notice that in this scripture it talks about how opposition arose because of grace? Just because you tap into the fountain of grace does not mean that you will instantly be in Candy Land. Opposition and brokenness will come, but it is in those moments that His grace is sufficient. It is in our moments of opposition and struggle that we grow, discover and reap wisdom. We reap great wisdom and intimacy with God if we cling to Him instead of turning our backs on Him during those moments. He promises that he will never leave us but sometimes in our broken places instead of seeing the beauty of grace we only see the broken, and we run and hide in our sin, shame and doubt.

When we forget about the grace, we run into the arms of the enemy and begin the dance of death. This is a result of the power of life being drained from us when we disconnect for the fountain. You may be thinking: where can I find the kind of grace that produces such remarkable things? It can only be found in the cross of Christ. When Jesus went to the cross, he bled a fountain of grace for you. This fountain flowed as he was beaten until he was unrecognizable. This fountain flowed when he had his head cut with a crown of thorns. This fountain flowed when he had his hands and feet pierced with nails and when his side was cut open. It sounds gruesome, and I can only imagine what that sight looked like. I think about the time that I fell and cut my knee open while I was dancing in the rain. My knee bled all over the place. I ran into the house to get a rag to stop the flow, but I left a trail of blood the whole way as I ran. My knee had produced enough blood to leave a trail. Can you imagine the trail left by Jesus? His trail was not only blood! It was grace for all of us who will see it and receive it. That is why there is power in the blood of Jesus; it is all because of the grace that it represents. There is grace in that blood.

The grace that Jesus let flow from himself for us, now must be the grace we let flow from our lives into others. We must be the fountain; a fountain that never runs dry. What flow are you giving others? The flow that grace produces or the flow that unforgiveness produces?

The opposite of grace is unforgiveness and judgement. When we stop the flow of grace, we get everything that is opposite of it. Look up the scriptures below to see what unforgiveness/lack of grace will produce in your life.

- Luke 18:10-14 _____

- Hebrews 10:28-31 _____

- Matthew 13:13-15 _____

- Matthew 6:14-15 _____

Unforgiveness will produce a lack of justification, judgement, lack of vision, lack of hearing, lack of understanding and unforgiveness from your father in heaven. In broken moments there are times when we house unforgiveness towards others and ourselves. Unforgiveness creates a fountain that no one wants to drink from because it flows with negative thoughts, which lead to negative emotions, and then to negative actions.

When you are in the cycle of unforgiveness, it becomes a pattern that only forgiveness can stop.

CYCLE OF UNFORGIVENESS

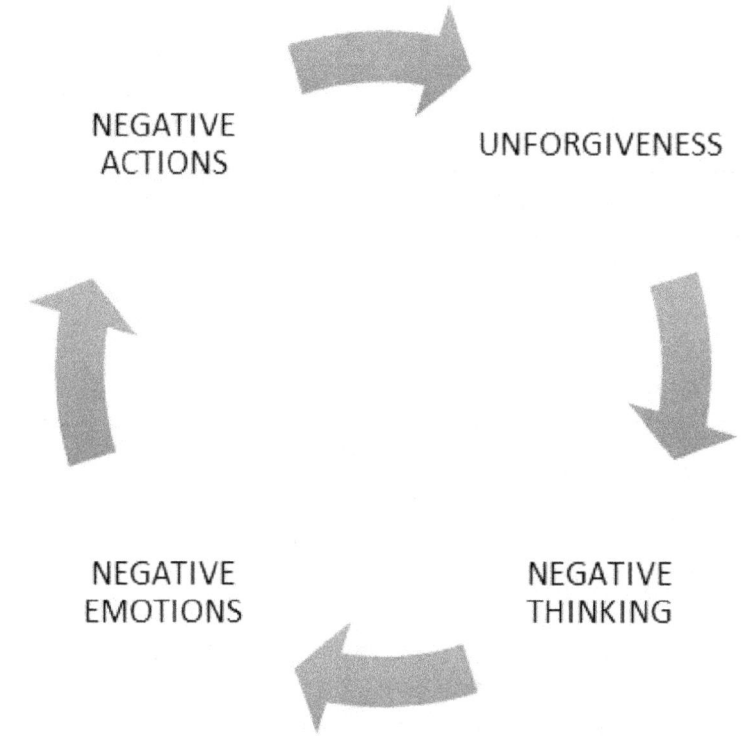

Who or what has put you on the unforgiveness wheel that keeps spinning your life out of control? When you are on the wheel of unforgiveness, it is like a vicious cycle, it always starts with unforgiveness then it leads to negative actions. These negative actions then will lead to creating other opportunities for hurt and unforgiveness to occur. Again, it is like a Ferris wheel that will not stop spinning. Eventually sickness, dizziness, and exhaustion set in. You become disoriented with life and even with the reason to live.

Have you ever heard the saying that weak people walk in unforgiveness? This is a statement that I want to contest. Christ says, *"It is in our weakness that His power is made known."* Weakness is not a terrible thing when you focus on the fact that it is in your weakness that Christ dwells. When we think we are strong within ourselves, pride is produced, which then brings unforgiveness and a desire for vengeance. When we see our weakness as being a strength, we understand that we cannot walk our forgiveness out by ourselves, but Christ can do it through us as we surrender to Him.

The only thing we need to do is give everything over to God and know that He will take care of it for us. Let His fountain of grace take over and drown out all negative thoughts, negative emotions, and negative actions. When you think and dwell on Christ what does it produce? Do this all throughout your day. Get a scripture that you can think of every time a negative thought comes up in your mind. One that is often used is found in Philippians 4:4-9, which says,

"Rejoice in the Lord always. I will say it again: Rejoice! [praise] Let your gentleness be evident to all. The Lord is near. Do not be anxious [negative emotion] about anything, but in everything with prayer and petition, with thanksgiving, present your request to God. And the peace of God, which transcends all understanding, will guard your hearts and your minds in Christ's Jesus [fountain of grace].

Finally, brothers and sisters, whatever is true, whatever is noble, whatever is right, whatever is pure, whatever is lovely, whatever is admirable—if anything is excellent or praiseworthy [thankfulness] think about such things [thoughts]. Whatever you have learned or received or heard from me or see in me- put it into practice [action]. And the God of peace will be with you."

This is Paul's writing, and in it he is saying *listen guys, if you will begin to walk in a positive thought pattern followed by positive actions, you will have great peace even in a storm.* This scripture explains the cycle of peace and forgiveness.

A thought going through your mind right now might be that you do not want to forgive. If this is the case, I understand because I was there at one point on my journey. I didn't want to forgive because inside I knew if I forgave my ex-husband and the pastor of the church, I was in for 18 years, then that would be the end because I would release them. I didn't want the end to come. The thought of it being the end caused me to hold on to the only thing that I had control over, which was unforgiveness. The unforgiveness was in my hands, and no one could steal that piece of the relationship from me unless I decided. I also thought that my unforgiveness brought pain to the other person involved, but it was only a weight that was holding me in a place away from the cross.

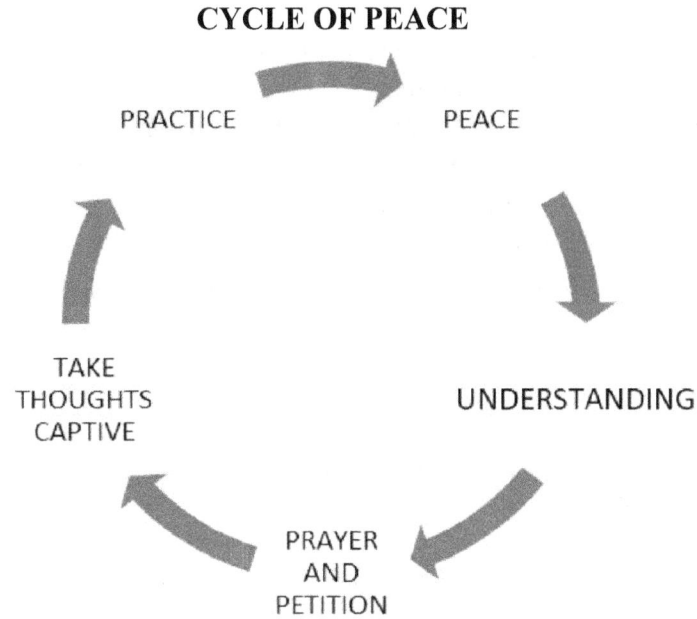

CYCLE OF PEACE

The cycle of peace and forgiveness can come! It is possible when you realize that peace only comes from an understanding that it has nothing to do with you. Paul says, *"Rejoice in the LORD always."* Then he repeats it, *"Again I say rejoice!"* with an exclamation point. It is imperative to understand that God is the one with the fountain of grace and without being tapped into that fountain, grace cannot flow.

The next step in the cycle of peace is to pray and petition. I pray every day for the people that hurt me—the ones that hurt me on purpose and the ones that have hurt me without knowing. It is important to get into the habit of praying when you feel hurt or offended by someone. Paul says, *"Be anxious for nothing but approach everything with pray and petition."* The definition of "petition" is to make or present a request to authority regarding a certain cause.

Prayer is defined as a solemn request for help, or an expression of thanks expressed to God or an object of worship. So, prayer includes being thankful for all of who God is, and what He produces in your life. The brokenness is worth giving God thanks for because it will produce greatness in our lives if we let it.

The first chapter of James, in the Bible, says that we should have pure joy in our broken moments because it develops perseverance which then creates maturity, which makes you complete and creates provision. You are beautifully broken my friend, and goodness can flow from your painful wounds and scars when you are tapped into the fountain. Take a moment to pray. It may be very difficult to start off the prayer, so use this outline if you are struggling.

Dear God,
Please help me to forgive _____ (fill in the blank with the names of people who have hurt and offended you). Help me to care and love you enough that in return I love people enough to forgive them the way you forgave me. Thank you for every moment of my life—the good, the bad and the ugly. I know that in them all, you grow me and make me more like you. In Jesus' name, amen.

Now it is time to capture every thought that may be contrary to what you just prayed and petitioned God for. The Message Bible puts Paul's words like this: *"Summing it all up, friends, I'd say you'll do best by filling your minds and meditating on things true, noble, reputable, authentic, compelling, gracious—the best, not the worst; the beautiful, not the ugly, things to praise, not things to curse."* This sums up what your thoughts should be in your brokenness. Is it easy? Nope, but remember that it is in our weakness that God's strength and fountain of grace are found.

This grace leads to the last step in the cycle of peace, which is practice. Sometimes things are so hard that it takes practice to be able to walk it out. All the greats must practice what they want to be great at doing. The great basketball star doesn't win a game and then stop practicing. The great gymnast doesn't win a medal when they stop practicing. The talented artist doesn't get one painting sold and stop practicing. They each must keep practicing to produce bigger and better results. They don't achieve a goal and then stop practicing.

You may pray, petition and think right one day and obtain peace. Then the next day comes, and you think the peace will carry over. It doesn't—you must get on the cycle of peace daily. Think about a Ferris wheel: when it stops, you are stuck, and you only get to the finish line when there is movement. Make sure that you are moving so that you can obtain the ticket to the fountains of grace that produce the peace and strength to forgive.

The one person I struggled the most to present grace and forgiveness to was myself. I was so mad at myself for the sin that I got caught up in. I was a youth pastor—I was not supposed to allow sin to be a part of who I was. I had become an angry person inside because I had jumped on the cycle of unforgiveness towards myself. This cycle led me to believe that I could never be used by God again. I began to act like God had never seen my past failures and loved me enough to forgive me. We should allow ourselves to understand that the fountain of grace covers our sins and ridiculousness too. There is enough grace for all our failures.

REALITY RECALL

By Pastor Christie Lyerla

This recall is by the pastor that I hurt with my actions in Florida. This pastor loved and showed me grace like I had never seen. It was this fountain of grace that she presented to me that drew me back to my calling and the mission God had for me.

In this current generation and the American culture, grace is a word that is thrown around quite a bit. Entire ministries are built around this one word. But one doesn't appreciate the true value of this term until they are required to "extend grace" to someone else. Receiving grace may seem easy but extending grace will cost you something.

This was my personal experience after walking through a betrayal—one of many. This one was very personal and extremely painful. But like always, God gave me the grace to push forward. Walking through this situation brought me to one of my favorite verses: 2 Corinthians 12:9 (NIV) *"My Grace is sufficient for you, for my strength is made perfect in weakness."*

I have quoted that verse so many times in my life. But when asked to extend grace to someone else, I found myself faced with a true difficulty. I found out that I only have grace for today. Betrayal occurs so much to people in ministry. It causes one to find it difficult to trust people. I don't trust a lot of people. When a person you fully trust seems to turn on you, it can shake you to your core—or at least it had that effect on me. I felt physically sick. I was so distraught with the situation at hand.

After time passed, I had the opportunity to extend grace and forgiveness in this situation. I say opportunity because that is exactly what it was. It wasn't an obligation, but God had to bring healing to me and someone else. When we give forgiveness, two people receive freedom: the person extending forgiveness and the one being forgiven.

When one looks into the face of a person asking for forgiveness with true humility and brokenness, there is no other option but to forgive. Although healing is a process, I feel it begins at the moment of extending grace to another. I did find out that extending grace requires wisdom. Do you open your home to that rebellious teenager that has no place to go? Do you keep loving that person that has a history of deception and telling lies, knowing that one day that deception may be turned against you? Do you trust a person who has turned on you? In each given situation, God gives His wisdom, direction and strength to walk victoriously in order to represent Him well.

Will we be grace personified? Grace that is real? Will we walk the walk and not just talk or preach about it? Will we be a living grace that is not just preached from a pulpit? I experienced the joy and the difficulty that extending grace brings. I can say personally that it is worth it!

MEDITATION MOMENT

STILL MOMENT
Set the timer for 4 minutes and rest in the understanding that God has forgiven you for all that you have done and not done, and God will be your strength to forgive others.

PRAYER
God,

At this moment, please help me to get on the cycle of peace by understanding that your Fountain of Grace is for me and everyone that will tap into it. I pray that today and every day I will take my thoughts captive and surrender them to you. I will practice what is preached in your word. Your word is what will bring life to my bones and what will help to repair the broken state that I am walking in. It is in your word and grace that I can become beautiful even in my brokenness. Thank you so much for your grace and love that is never-ending for me.

In Jesus' name, amen.

WORD
This meditation moment comes from the Acts 6 & 7. It is about one of the greatest examples of grace. Stephen was a man that was chosen by the disciples to be in a select group of seven men to help with the distribution of food. They appointed him to this task so that they could focus on the word and prayer for the people. In Acts 6:5 it states that *"Stephen was a man full of faith and of the Holy Spirit."* In verse 8 it says, *"He was a man, full of God's grace, power, he performed great wonders and signs among the people."* Stephen was a man doing wonderful things for God and still…God's chosen one, though walking in grace, would suffer persecution and brokenness. Stephen had many come against him speaking lies about him. Stephen was brought before the Sanhedrin (an assembly of men appointed over every city in Israel). A false

witness testified that Stephen was saying that Jesus will destroy the temple and change the customs of Moses (the customs of the Jewish people). In this meeting, Stephen, full of grace and power, began to testify about God. His speech must have gone on for a while because he told the whole story from Abraham to Jesus. At the end of his speech, he says in Acts 7:51(NIV), *"You stiff-necked people, with uncircumcised hearts and ears! You are just like your fathers: you always resist the Holy Spirit."*

You can imagine the anger that began to burn in the assembly. They became furious. In the midst of their frustration, Stephen looked up to heaven and said to the people, *"Look, I see heaven and the son of man standing at the right hand of God."* At this the people covered their ears and yelled at the top of their voices, they rushed Stephen and stoned him to death. While they were stoning him, he said, *"Lord Jesus, receive my spirit."* He then cried out, *"Lord, do not hold this sin against them."*

This is a story of a man in a *Beautifully Broken* moment, realizing if he stays tapped into the grace giver, he will be able to forgive. Instead, he brings great glory to God through his situation. Walk in that kind of grace today, the fountain of grace that others will be eager to drink from.

WORSHIP

Listen to the song "Grace" by Unspoken. This song says some call grace foolish and impossible, but that every heart it rescues is a miracle! Let your heart be rescued while you listen to this song.

LINK LEVERAGE TOOL

AWARENESS
- Write three words that stood out to you while reading this chapter.

ASK
- Ask yourself what did these words speak to you?

GOAL
- Write down one goal that will help you to grow this week.

CHANGE
- What change can you make to acheive your goal?

SERVE
- Who did I serve this week and how did it make me feel?

ILLUMINATION

Use this journal to write three valuable nuggets that you learned in this chapter and how you have won in life because of them. Then write three things you are thankful for. Look for the light in your darkness.

_____
_____
_____
_____
_____
_____
_____
_____
_____
_____
_____
_____
_____
_____
_____
_____
_____
_____
_____
_____
_____
_____
_____
_____
_____
_____
_____

Grace displayed is forgiveness walked out.

Use this page to draw what is on your mind, write out scriptures that stand out or quotes that speak to you.

STEP 5
RESPOND TO THE STRIP DOWN

It is in the moments of vulnerability that true relationship can be born.

AFRESH

I bet the phrase "strip it down" is not exactly what you expected to see in this book called *Beautifully Broken*. When I thought about this chapter, I thought about the song by Luke Bryan. The lyrics say, *strip it down, strip it down like it used to be*. This song is about a couple that had grown apart, but they are stripping things down so that they can regain the intimacy they once had for each other. This is what this chapter will be all about— the stripping down. Often in our brokenness, we divert, not to God, but to the things of this world that can bring us comfort. Addiction, success, food, and relationships are common things we try to soak ourselves in. We do this so that we can cover up the pain of our past or our present. Are you ready to strip it down?

We strip it down all the time in the natural sense, but what does stripping it down in the spiritual sense mean and what does it produce? If you strip it down in the bedroom with a spouse, it produces intimacy. If you strip it down in the doctor's office, you get an examination. If you strip it down in the bathroom, you get a release or a refreshing. When you respond to the strip down from God, it will produce the same things:

Intimacy, examination, release and a refreshing.

The Bible provides a list of things we may use to cover up our brokenness. It can be found in Galatians 5:19 (NIV) which says *"Acts of flesh are obvious: sexual immorality, impurity, and debauchery; idolatry and witchcraft; hatred, discord, jealousy, fits of rage, selfish ambition, dissensions, factions, and envy; drunkenness, orgies and the like."* This scripture goes on to say that those that walk in these ways will not inherit the kingdom of God.

There were many times as a child when my mom would say to me, "Naked you came into this world and naked you will leave this world." I think that Jesus is saying this to us today but with a different tone. He is saying, "Baby girl, I brought you into this world with nothing to hide and this is how I want to deliver you out of this world." God wants nothing but the best for us. He has so many promises that He is so eager to give to you, and one of those promises is freedom.

There is brokenness that we must contend with because of the brokenness in the garden. The struggle can be found in the book of Genesis in the Bible. It started off with "Do I eat it or not?" Eve was stripped originally. She was naked in the garden. She was pure and had nothing to hide. The only time she was ready to put on a cover was when she felt she had something to hide. In Genesis, Eve was instructed not to eat of the forbidden tree and in verse 3:6 (NIV) it says, *"When Eve saw that the fruit of the tree was good for food and pleasing to the eye, and desirable for gaining wisdom, she took some and ate it."* She ate the one thing that was forbidden. She also decided she didn't want to walk the journey alone, so she gave some to her husband. They instantly made coverings because they saw that they were exposed for others to see. They felt because they had sinned and had been disobedient that they needed to try to cover up.

Is this what we do in our sin and brokenness? We try to hide from God and others what we are doing and how we feel when all along God knows and sees all. You cannot hide from God, so you might as well strip it down and let Him cover you up with His fountain of grace that we talked about in the last chapter. What are the things that, like Eve, make you feel like you need to cover up and hide?

_____

_____

_____

_____

Jesus is the only cover up we need. Everything else just needs to be stripped from our lives. There was a woman in the Bible that understood this to the fullest. She was a woman that others were ready to stone, but Jesus said to the woman he would cover her and protect her from being exposed to the wrong things. This woman's story is found in John 8:1-11 where it says that Jesus went to the Mount of Olives. At dawn, He appeared in the temple courts, where people were gathered all around him, and He sat down to teach them. He was approached by the Pharisees about a woman that was caught in adultery. They made this woman stand naked and exposed for all to see. They asked Jesus what they should do with her. The whole time they are trying to trap Jesus. Jesus at a certain point bent down and began to write in the sand. As Jesus continued to write in the sand, they kept questioning him. The Bible says that Jesus straightened up, and he flexed on them with this statement, *"Let any one of you who is without sin be the first to throw a stone at her."* When the Pharisees heard this, they began to walk away one by one. Jesus then asked the woman, *"Woman, where are they? Has no one condemned you?"* *"No one, sir,"* she said. *"Then neither do I condemn you,"* Jesus declared. *"Go now and leave your life of sin."*

Jesus wants to have an encounter where you expose yourself and all your sin to Him so that He can cover it with the blood of forgiveness and His grace. He is not ready to beat you up, call you out or throw you out. He is willing and ready to love you and breathe life into you. This woman had to surrender to the words of Jesus.

It is time that we allow Jesus to write in the sand of our hearts with His love. The way to do this is the same way that this young lady did it:

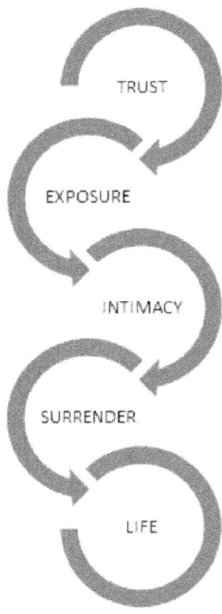

The woman in this story had to trust that Jesus was on her side. I am sure that with the life she was living she had been hurt so much that it was hard for her to trust. Learning to trust is one of the hardest parts of the journey in the strip down. How can I trust again? This woman could have said to Jesus, "You are just like them. You will eventually judge me and hurt me." Or she could throw herself out there and say it is worth a try. She didn't do anything fancy to trust Jesus, she just walked in faith, jumped into His love and His gallons of grace.

The second thing she did was stand there exposed. These men said to Jesus, "This woman stands here a sinner." The story does not say that she combatted the men by saying she wasn't doing what they accused her of. She just stood there exposed and let Jesus see who she was. You don't stand exposed and not become intimate with someone. Jesus and this woman had an encounter with each other. She knew that he was safe because in that intimate moment, Jesus treated here with gentleness, love, care and concern. Jesus will do the same with you as you have an intimate encounter with Him.

This woman then felt comfortable enough to surrender to the idea that she was clean and that Jesus was the life she was looking for to free her from the accusations and failures of her past. Begin to walk in this same kind of freedom today as you allow God to strip off the very thing that is holding you back from seeing the beauty in your broken places and that intense love He has for you.

REALITY RECALL

By Linda Orange

It all began after my husband and I separated, and I was moving forward with a divorce. He was an alcoholic and addicted to pornography. His addiction rocked my world and made me feel like I was not worthy of intimacy, love, affection, or desire. His desires destroyed not only his life, but they broke every part of my self-worth as a woman.

The enemy waits for moments when we are broken and vulnerable to infiltrate our lives with his deception. At the time, I was a children church leader and had been attending the church for approximately six years. I loved God and believed that I was sold out to Him.

That was until I received a phone call that would change my life in ways that I could never have imagined or that I would allow to happen. The call was from my high school sweetheart. I met him when I was 16 years old and fell in love. We began living together when I was 18 years old, and we ended our relationship when I was 20. He was caught cheating, and I was tired of battling this behavior along with his addiction to drugs and alcohol.

As we began conversing over the telephone across three states, the enemy was pouring into me how I had messed up God's plan for my life in my youth. God had given me this man at a youthful age and I destroyed God's initial blessing by ending it and marrying not once, but twice since. There was no hope for me when it came to love; I had already ruined God's plan.

Still, coming through a divorce and feeling broken and not good enough, this man began to speak words to me that I had longed for years to hear. Daily we shared all that life had given us, and I started to think that God was restoring what the enemy took from me.

My flesh was so weak and my heart was so desperate for love and validation from people that it didn't take long for the deception to take root and we began a long-distance relationship traveling to see each other and spending time reminiscing about our younger days. Those visits became more entangled when we introduced intimacy into the relationship.

I was so ashamed of what I was doing. I knew it was wrong, but I felt like I was being validated again. I pulled away from my friends, my church, my family and I dove in feet first, then the full body. It wasn't long before we decided that the traveling back and forth was too much, and he relocated back to our home state and moved in with my two children and me. He said all the right things, and my memories of our childhood romance were of course so jaded considering who he presented himself to be now.

You see, in and out of high school he was a manipulative individual addicted to drugs and alcohol with a bad temper. Now, the man he was showing me was kind, gentle, mature—a good father and of course— and most importantly he was God-fearing and in love with his Savior. My divorce was not yet final, neither was his.

In my blindness, I also could not see the hurt that I was causing my soon-to-be ex-husband, his soon-to-be ex-wife, and our children. Even after we blended our families, I found myself falling further and further from the person I once was a Godfearing, tithe paying, church leader. I found myself deeper and deeper in despair even though I still contended God was giving me back what I messed up in my youth.

To please me, the new man in my life wanted us to join a new church, and we visited several, but none brought me the peace that I so desperately needed, and little did I realize at the time, no place ever would. The peace I needed could only be found in my relationship with Christ, my Savior, who I was running from blindly and crashing into at every turn.

Finally, he suggested, "Let's go back to the church you attended in the beginning." Though I had so much fear walking into that place and facing my pastors, I felt it was something that needed to be done. That next Sunday, we went to service. I was greeted with love and welcomed. I remember crying and thinking: How can they love me when I am walking in here with all this sin surrounding me? Over the next few weeks, in a vulnerable state, I once again began to hear God's voice. So clearly, He gave me instructions to attain my peace. He forgave me for what I had done, but I needed to end the sin.

I asked my partner to move out and into an apartment until we could make our relationship right through marriage. Reluctantly he agreed. As we secured an apartment close to my home, God began to reveal other things to me that needed to stop. One by one, I started to set boundaries, and as I did, the scales that once covered my eyes began to fall off. I began to see the spiritual battle that I was in, one that would either consume me or one that I would allow God to claim the victory over.

Ultimately, the relationship came to an end, and as I look back, it was the worst nine months of my life. It was long enough to give birth to lifelong consequences that God still helps me to overcome today.

MEDITATION MOMENT

STILL MOMENT
Rest in God's peace today. Set a timer for 5 minutes, lay down on your bed and let God touch your heart and prepare it to release all that is not of Him.

PRAYER
Dear God,

I come to you open and ready for the strip down. Help me with _____ (write out the area you are battling). God, I thank you that just like the woman in this story, you will cover me and love me through it all. Forgive me for all things I have let into my life and that have caused me to pull away from you. I don't want to try to hide anymore. Thank you for always standing with your arms open and loving me as I run into them.

In Jesus' name, amen.

WORD
John 4 is where the story from the word will come today. It is a story of a woman at a well— Jacob's well. Jesus was tired, thirsty and hungry so He sat at this well. While He was sitting there a Samaritan came to get water, and He said to her, *"Will you give me a drink?"* The Samaritan woman said, *"You are a Jew, and I am a Samaritan woman. How can you ask me for a drink?"* Jesus said, *"If you knew the gift of God and who it is that was asking for a drink, you would have asked Him, and He would have to give you living water."* The woman said, *"Where can I get this living water?"* Jesus told the woman, *"Whoever drinks the living water will never thirst again."* She responded with, *"Sir, give me this water so that I won't get thirsty and have to keep coming here to draw water."* Jesus told the woman to go and get her husband. She replied that she doesn't have a husband. Jesus said to her, *"You are right when you say you have no husband. The fact is, you have had five husbands, and the man you now have is not your husband. What you have just said is*

quite true." This story goes on and talks about other things with the disciples, but I want to pick back up in verse 39 because it says that *"Many Samaritans from the town believed because of this woman's testimony."* This woman was exposed and then covered by God's love in a way that drew others to Jesus.

In our brokenness, a lot of times we will respond to Jesus like this woman at the well did. We will make excuses as to why Jesus cannot come into our lives in a personal and intimate way. Jesus comes to us and says, "Let me have your stuff, let me strip you of the mess." We say, "You are Jesus, and I am a drug addict, prostitute, adulterer, glutton, etc. these do not mix with who you are." So, we pretend and try to hide from God. That is exactly what this woman did initially, and He called her out because He knew that he had the answer for her. He knew that His living water was what she needed to cleanse her.

Don't be afraid of the strip down! It is in the moments of vulnerability that true relationship can be born.

WORSHIP

Listen to the song "What a Beautiful Name" by Hillsong Worship. This song talks about the beautiful name of Jesus and how good He is, in addition to how His name is powerful, and nothing can stand against it. Know that as you call on His name nothing will stand against it in the strip down.
You will be FREE.

LINK LEVERAGE TOOL

AWARENESS
- Write three words that stood out to you while reading this chapter.

ASK
- Ask yourself what did these words speak to you?

GOAL
- Write down one goal that will help you to grow this week.

CHANGE
- What change can you make to acheive your goal?

SERVE
- Who did I serve this week and how did it make me feel?

ILLUMINATION

Use this journal to write three valuable nuggets that you learned in this chapter and how you have won in life because of them. Then write three things you are thankful for. Look for the light in your darkness.

*"Then **you will know** the **truth**, and the **truth will set you free**."*

Use this page to draw what is on your mind, write out scriptures that stand out or quotes that speak to you.

STEP 6
REALIGN

Rewarding relationships will always draw out the beauty in our broken.

AFRESH

Pain often will lead you into the wrong arms. It is imperative that you align yourself with the right people in the right avenues to achieve enormous success in your journey of being *Beautifully Broken*. The enemy will lure you into his arms in your moments of weakness if you are not careful.

What is the first thought you have when you think of the word align? Is it the alignment of a car? I am not a mechanic, but in my research, I discovered that an alignment refers to an adjustment of the vehicle's suspension—this is the system that connects a vehicle to its wheels. It is a very important process for a vehicle running correctly. When a car is aligned, the car will go in the direction that the driver is directing it to go. If it is not aligned the wheels will point in the wrong direction, and it will be hard to control the vehicle.

When we are walking in a world of pain, it is possible that our alignment will come out of balance. It is imperative to figure this out and get it fixed immediately. When your car is not properly aligned, it will have some negative effects on the car as a whole. The steering will be off, and you will feel the car pulling to the left or the right. If you feel that life is pulling you to the left or the right and there is confusion on where you are going, know that your alignment may be off.

Another effect is that the suspension is off. What happens when the suspension is going bad in a car? It becomes very hard to stop and turn the car. It causes "nose dives" when the car stops, it rides rough and causes the car to drift. Does any of this sound familiar to your life?

One of the most important things affected when the car is out of alignment is safety. The lack of being able to control the car's direction causes it to end up in places you never intended for it to go. Lack of proper alignment can cause you to put yourself in dangerous positions.

In life, when you are not aligning with the right cause or people it can cause these same effects. In our lives we hit potholes, we struggle, have setbacks and potentially begin to veer to the left or right. We disconnect from the ones that our alignment should be with—the people and places that will lead us to the right destinations in life.

The first part of realigning is with God. You can never go in the right direction without first aligning with him. You can refer back to the section titled "Salvation" in the introduction of this book. Remember, His grace is what will lead you to the proper connection with Him. When you align with what Jesus did on the cross and tap into His fountains of grace, many blessings and great beauty will come your way even in the middle of the struggle and brokenness.

The second part of realigning is one we have not discussed in detail yet, it is the alignment with good, godly people. This alignment makes the ride of life a little easier. When you hit the potholes of life while aligned with the right people, they help guide you to remain balanced and focus on your path. My pastor, Dave Sumrall, says all the time "Show me your friends and I will show you your future." What exactly does he mean by this? It is vital to your victory for you to understand this concept. So, let us dive into the Bible and see the depth of this statement.

First look in your Bible at the scripture found in Proverbs 18:24. What does it say about this?

_____
_____
_____
_____
_____

In this scripture God is saying that we need to choose our friends—those we align with—closely and with wisdom. We need to know that not everyone that we associate with should be someone that we let into the intimate parts of our lives. We should always be looking for the quality in a friend, not the quantity of friends.

In today's culture, it is typical, to let anyone and everyone in our circle because social media tells us that we need to accept all friend requests. If we accept everyone, we can display our popularity to the world. We even base our self-worth on how many friends we have and how many likes we get.

We often invite people in our circle of alignment that should not even be there. With this statement, do not misunderstand me, we need to love all people! But aligning and loving are two different things. Remember what the alignment on a car does, it leads you in the right direction. The Bible says in Proverbs 4:27, *"Do not turn to the right or the left; keep your feet from evil."*

Now look up Proverb 13:20 and write down what it says about aligning with the right people.

_____
_____
_____
_____

It states that if you spend time together with the wise you become wise, but if you hang out with the fools you will suffer harm. When you align with the fool you begin to act like a fool. A fool is someone that will lead you deeper into pain and further away from your God. Proverbs 22:24-25 (MSG) says, *"Don't hang out with angry people; don't keep company with hotheads. Bad temper is contagious—don't get infected by it."*

Let's see what Proverbs 27:9 states. Jot down your understanding of this scripture:

_____
_____
_____
_____

This scripture lets you know that when you mix with the right people it is like a sweet aroma that makes your heart happy. It also says that the sweetness of a friend comes from his earnest counsel.

As you seek Christ about your alignments, ask him if you have aligned with people that have caused you to be off balance. You may have some friends that are benefitting you and some that may be hindering you. Ask God to reveal to you which friends are giving off a bad aroma. God may encourage you to remove yourself from some relationships that are not taking you into a positive light.

REALIGN

Know that anything you are willing to give up for God, He is willing to replace with something even better. Let Him create the alignments/friendships you need in your life.

I love Florida and visit it often. Every time I go, there are two things that I want while I am there. I want a really good avocado and a mango fresh from the tree. My cousin asked me one time, "How do you know if the mango is good or not?" I told her I always smell it and if it gives off a sweet aroma, I know that it is one I want to bite into. This is the way it will be when you align yourself again or for the first time with rewarding relationships.

Last, but not least, look up Proverbs 27:17 and write down your thoughts:

_____
_____
_____
_____

This states that iron will sharpen iron, and one man sharpens another. It is important to have the alignment with a friend that will be honest with you above all else. When a friend is honest sometimes it can feel like a sharp knife in your heart but the surgery that the sharp knife is doing will make you a better person for God and for the world. It will help you to remove the debris in your life and create a different momentum.

I have two friends that I have aligned with that have been with me through every one of my beautifully broken moments. One I have been friends with since my sophomore year of high school and the other for 21 years. These ladies continuously challenge me to think higher, to shine brighter and to love deeper. They do not let me stay in my brokenness. They pull me higher by sharpening me with the Word and encouragement. Sharpening may come in different forms, but you need to align with a friend that is not just going to sharpen you with kindness. There are times in our brokenness that we are walking in a realm of pity, unforgiveness, and discouragement. In this state, we need someone to be honest with us. Aligning with the right friendships will bring a steady flow of growth and guidance birthed out of honesty.

The next alignment, we need to evaluate is our alignment with a cause. The Bible in John 15:13 (NIV) states *"Greater love has no one than this: to lay down one's life for one's friend."* When I think of this scripture, it makes me think of my son and the alignment he made with the world as he signed up for the Navy. We align ourselves daily with people, groups, and causes that we believe in. My son chose to align with the cause of fighting for our country. He chose to fight for freedom. I knew that my son had an awesome calling in his life. I thought he would be a pastor someday. When he was just six years-old, he would preach to the students at camps. When he signed up for the Navy, he said: "I am going to serve the cause of freedom for the world."

This decision to align with the cause of freedom for our country was not chosen lightly. Choosing him was not something the Navy took lightly either. Our country put my son through a rigorous process of testing. They tested him physically, academically and mentally. During the testing, they were evaluating him to see if he was willing to commit to aligning with the USA to fight at all costs. During this process, he was required to learn pledges, taught how to salute the flag, taught how to honor authority, and so much more. He learned what sacrifice meant as he entered boot camp. My son was aligning with the country to gain support and give support. What cause have you aligned with?

Don't align with the cause of broken but beauty. We align so many times with our pain, and it pressures us to fight for the cause of pain rather than fighting for the cause of life. In pain, it is important to align yourself with a cause, understand the cause, and walk out the cause.

This is where a church alignment is important. When you align with a church, don't align with any church. The Bible says that in the last days there will be many that are deceived. In my brokenness, I aligned with ITOWN and small groups that were connected to ITOWN. This is where I found a group of individuals that taught me to trust, love and serve again.

As a previous youth pastor of a church, I learned that doing life alone was common for people in my position. There were a lot of things that could not be discussed outside of the office. This created in me a desire to walk through things alone and allow my insides to try to handle everything without release.

When I started attending ITOWN one of the first concepts that seemed foreign to me was the statement that you should not do life alone. Jesus never intended for us to sit in a lonely spot. Being alone can open an opportunity for the enemy to distort your thinking, blur your vision and align you with the wrong cause. But when you have a shepherd and friends that will step in, surround you, and encourage you, you will walk in victory. The bible states that one can chase a thousand and two can chase ten thousand. It is important to have other believers on your side.

Scripture tells us in Hebrews 10:25 that, *"We should not give up on meeting together, as some are in the habit of doing, but encouraging one another—and all the more as we see the Day approaching."* When in proper alignment with a Bible-based church, you will get spiritual food that you can eat that will make you stronger. It will be a place you will be encouraged and learn new habits or be reminded of habits that you can do to help you see the beauty.

How many times have we stood and nonchalantly given our allegiance to the flag? Before my son joined the Navy, I would stand for the Pledge of Allegiance, but I never really understood the depth of what I was aligning with as I recited it. It was not until my son began to sacrifice his life for our country that I understood the depth of my pledge and the depth of what the flag represented.

The first time I experienced the reality of it was when Dylan walked into the recruiter's office to sign his final papers. When he entered, there was a flag to the right of the door. My son stopped and saluted the flag. I began to cry because it was in that moment that I understood the sacrifice of the allegiance to the flag. When he saluted, he was saying I align myself with the United States, and I pledge to align myself with all that it represents and all that it fights continuously for. It meant that he aligned himself with the authority of the country and the cause of freedom for all.

Photo credit to *Noel Photography*

When the flag was created, it was created with the intention to draw a nation together. Its colors represent valor, liberty, and justice. The pledge tells you exactly what you are aligning yourself with: It is the cause of liberty and justice for all.

Many people are walking around this world dead inside and emotionless because they don't understand their allegiance to the cause they are fighting for, or they have aligned with the one holding the death flag—a flag that draws us into self-hate, anger, and deception.

Flags, in general, serve as a rallying point. When I was a youth pastor every year at camp the first thing the youth would do is create a flag for their cabin. This flag would stand as a rallying point. Anytime the cabins would go from one activity to the next they would raise their flags high and march under the banner of what they were defined by. It was a representation of who they were aligned with and a way to rally the troops for a cause.

Capturing or stealing another cabin's flag was a highlight for all campers. They would wait for an opportunity to accomplish this goal. They would look for flags lying around not being protected, hanging but not being guarded, or even as you carelessly raised it up for your group. If your flag was stolen, it would bring confusion and chaos to the team. It would also create a desire within the groups to get it back.

This is what happens when we are in our brokenness without seeing a cause that we can align with. We become careless in our allegiance, and the enemy will swoop in and steal our identity and the connection to the ones that will help us to defeat him. John 10:10 states that *"He comes to kill, steal and destroy..."* The enemy has a huge task, and we surrender our allegiance to him in times of darkness and allow him to kill our dreams, to steal our hope and to destroy our vision. The second part of John 10:10 says *"I have come [Jesus talking] that you may have life and have it to the full."*

In war, if someone aligns with the enemy, they forfeit their rights and benefits with the side they were initially standing with. Light and dark cannot dwell together in one vein. You must choose this day which side you will align with. Will you align with the cause of darkness or the beauty of your brokenness? Aligning with the beauty of your brokenness will produce a desire for a cause that is beyond you. It will take you out of a selfish mode and put a desire in you that will bring life to others.

REALITY RECALL

By Nancy Adjohan

Me + You + Us = Beautiful

Barren is what I thought I was the day I sat on the toilet and felt the life that was inside of me slowly slip out. I did not even know if the baby was a boy or girl, I just knew that it was gone. The tears that I shed and the blood that was lost was the birth of death and not life. I thought this part of my life was over—you know, the broken part—the part that never saw the light at the end of the tunnel, just darkness. Yet there I was, in the dark, on the toilet as the life that was once inside of me slowly slipped out.

Really?! I thought to myself. Really God? This was your plan for me? Another testimony of something being taken away from me. And to you be the glory? Why? So that everyone can see that you are great? So that we can believe that when we, too, are taken away from this earth one day, we will meet those that passed way too soon? —like my son, or maybe it was my daughter. I did not hold your people captive, yet you stripped me away from my first born as if I did. Really?! Really, God?!

Outwardly, I showed signs of pregnancy, yet there was no baby. No one to nurse, love and cherish. The tiny shoes that we had already purchased did not have feet to be placed on. The emptiness that we felt could not be filled. I had never felt so inadequate in my life. I felt as if I failed my husband, my family, and all women. I could hear the scripture, "be fruitful and multiply," so the seed was planted, but it did not bear fruit. Out it came and down it went, and like a tree that was commanded to shrivel up and die, it was gone.

I tried to keep it together as much as I could as we drove to the hospital. They must take away what remains as if a baby comes in pieces. I laid on the hospital bed broken. I woke up from my surgery, broken. I went home, broken.

Now and then I would look for my baby. Then I would remember that I am no longer pregnant. I guess it was difficult because I knew that for me not to be pregnant anymore that meant there had to be a birth. Life was inside of me, and now it should be in my arms, but it was not. He, or maybe she, was not. And the joy that I once felt was gone, just like my baby. And the room that was set up in my heart for my little one was now ablaze with my fear, anger, hurt and brokenness.

What now? What to do when you feel like your Heavenly Father has rejected you like your worldly father. What do you do when you feel like you have done all that you can to live a righteous life, yet keep getting kicked, punched, and dragged? What do you do when you feel like you cannot stand on faith? What do you do when you do not want to curse God, but you do not want to worship Him either? What do you do when you feel like the only thing you have are questions with no answers? Eventually, you end up sinking—sinking into your brokenness hoping that God will save you before you drown and that is when it happens: Beauty.

I did not experience that beauty right away. It took a long time for me to stop asking questions and trust God, trust that where he had me is where He wanted me to be even though I did not understand. I had to trust that the plans that He had for me were good even when it felt like He was against me. There were times I did not know if God was here to kill, steal and destroy or if it was the devil. Because even as God's child somehow, I was still losing so much. The more I thought about it though, the death of my firstborn did not save the world, but God's did. His son, my Jesus, was perfect in all His ways and even in His perfection received a death that He did not deserve. My son, maybe daughter, is a gift to God as His son was a gift to me. And who better to take care of such a precious gift than the almighty God! From there I saw the glory that is to be given to Him and thanked Him for trusting me as a vessel to carry a gift that belongs to Him. In knowing that, I knew a little more of who God is. He is trusting and loving and gives back what is taken from us, even if He is the one that has taken it from us. Does He not know better than I? That is one question that I can answer: Yes, He does.

My husband and I now have a beautiful son whom we love and adore. It was rocky for us as husband and wife for a while because I thought I let him down and unknowingly he felt powerless in it all. We did not talk about our feelings and went through life as if there was no tragedy. We went back to work; we ran errands, we paid bills, watched movies, and ate meals. Thoughts were kept separate, and so were tears. We argued about the smallest things, without realizing that it was because of our loss. Upon arguing one day, we sat down and faced the reality that our child was gone. It is ok to grieve together, and that we did. It is ok to pray together, and that we did. It is ok to survive and move forward, and that we did. I love my husband with all my heart and thank God that it is not just my brokenness but his, and that our marriage did not break.

In this life, beauty is not just our clothes, makeup, and hair extensions—it is seeing God not only in the joys of life but also in the tribulations. It is linking arms with the ones you love and not letting go despite the winds that shake you.

Brokenness may crack your foundation, but beauty is standing firm as God repairs the cracks, sealing it with His promises that will not fail us. Oh, how beautiful our God is.

MEDITATION MOMENT

STILL MOMENT

Sit still for six minutes and think about your relationships that you are in right now, the causes that you are aligned with and the depth of your relationship with Jesus. Let God reveal to you any relationships that need to be repaired, removed or rewarded.

PRAYER
God,

I pray that you would create in me a pure heart. One that will seek you for guidance on rewarding relationships and for the cause that you want me to align with. It is important for me to denounce all relationships that I have created that are not of you and to reward and press into all relationships that you have brought into my life. Please help me to see all relationships with pure eyes and a soft heart.

In Jesus' name, amen.

WORD

The length of time you wait to fix the alignment on a car will determine the magnitude of damage. Tires will wear out and you will have a tough time maintaining control of the car. This is how Ruth in the Bible must have felt. She had lost her husband and was heading back to her mother-in-law's land with her. Naomi, the mother-in-law, said, *"I can never produce for you another son so please stay here in your land and do not come with me."* This statement was directed to Ruth and to Orpah, who were the wives of her sons. Orpah chose to leave and go back. Ruth decided she was to be aligned with Naomi and nothing was going to take her away from that connection that God had created for her. She told Naomi, *"Don't ask me to leave you and turn back. Wherever you go, I will go; wherever you live, I will live. Your people will be my people, and your God will be my God."* Ruth let Naomi know that she was not going to let the pain and brokenness of her loss lead her to align with the wrong relationships and a wrong cause. She knew her destiny and beauty were wrapped up in the accountability, direction, wisdom and the encouragement of Naomi.

Ruth was right because the story carries on and she stays connected to Naomi and in return gets the blessing of Boaz. Ruth would have never connected to her divine future if she had not stayed aligned and focused. Boaz was not just a man, what he brought to Ruth in their relationship was so much more than just "a man." God brought provision, favor, and redemption to Ruth through this man. God has the people He wants you to align with and stay aligned with so that he can pour out His promises on you. Rewarding relationships will always draw out the beauty of our brokenness.

WORSHIP

Listen to "Endless Friend" by Rachel Morrison and Matt Lesh. Christ is the most rewarding friendship you will have. When you cling to friends that cling to Him, you will tap into all that His friendship brings with them. Listen to this song and get a deep understanding of an endless friend.

LINK LEVERAGE TOOL

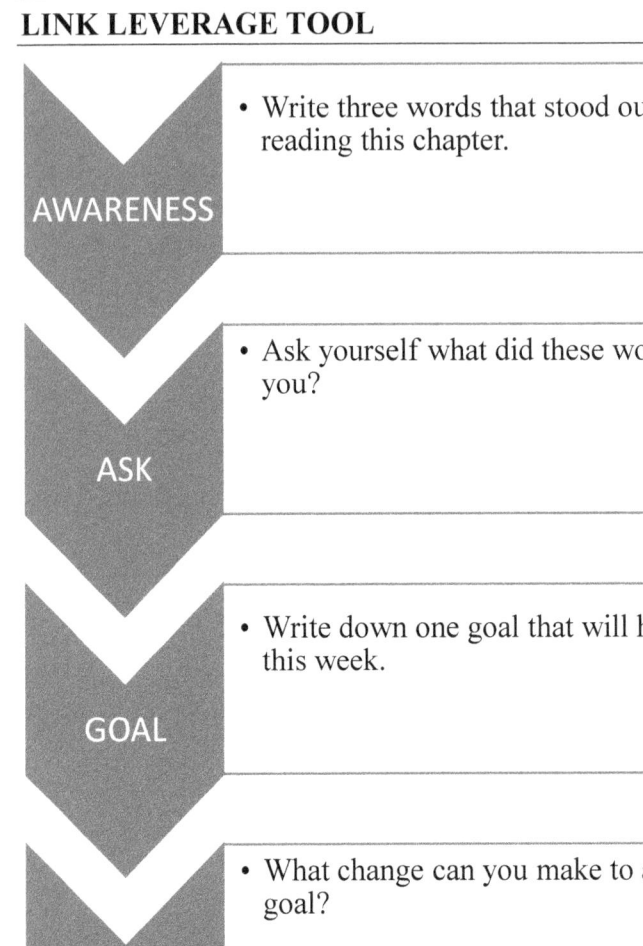

AWARENESS
- Write three words that stood out to you while reading this chapter.

ASK
- Ask yourself what did these words speak to you?

GOAL
- Write down one goal that will help you to grow this week.

CHANGE
- What change can you make to acheive your goal?

SERVE
- Who did I serve this week and how did it make me feel?

ILLUMINATION

Use this journal to write three valuable nuggets that you learned in this chapter and how you have won in life because of them. Then write three things you are thankful for. Look for the light in your darkness.

_____
_____
_____
_____
_____
_____
_____
_____
_____
_____
_____
_____
_____
_____
_____
_____
_____
_____
_____
_____
_____
_____
_____
_____
_____
_____
_____

Rewarding relationships help you to fulfill the journey with direction, encouragement and accountability. Embrace them!

Use this page to draw what is on your mind, write out scriptures that stand out or quotes that speak to you.

STEP 7
REARM

When you clothe yourself with God's armor and praise, you will win every battle.

AFRESH

Once you have aligned yourself with right forces, you will need to suit up for the battle. The enemy will be in an all-out war to create insecurity, fear, and doubt in you. Do not fall into his trap. Armor up so that you can be victorious in this new battle for your soul and future. God has new armor that He wants to give you.

When my son joined the Navy and went to boot camp, they gave them a ball cap with the wording "Recruit." My son was proud of that hat and wore it with honor. That was until he realized that there was a better hat that represented much more and would come with more power and gear. Many that were marching alongside him in boot camp would not make it through the entire process. They dropped out due to the intensity of the program. So, when it came to the end of boot camp, there was a ceremony for the ones that did make it. My son said this was the most rewarding and emotional part of boot camp. The ceremony started off with the playing of "Taps" on a very loud speaker. As the song was playing, the sergeant came to each sailor that had made it through the entire boot camp and put a hat on them that read "Sailor" instead of "Recruit." Dylan said, "There were not many dry eyes in the house at this time."

That day was the day that signified that my son was capable of wearing the armor that is set out to protect the sailor while he is in battle. The armor may not seem like a lot, but each piece of it has a specific purpose.

God has given us a clear understanding of what our armor is in the Word. We have armor to cover us from head to toe, and then there is the armor that we give to God. There is also an armor we receive with our praise and worship. In 2 Chronicles 20, Jehoshaphat was in an intense battle with the Moabites and Ammonites and some from Mount Seir. The Bible says, *"They waged war against Jehoshaphat."* It goes on to say that Jehoshaphat and his people were instructed not to be afraid because the Lord was going to fight their battle. They were instructed to *"Take up their position; stand firm and see the deliverance the Lord will give you."* Their position was in worship and praise. Jehoshaphat immediately bowed down with his face to the ground and all the people of Judah and Jerusalem fell down in worship. He began to appoint people to sing and to praise God for his splendor saying: *"Give thanks to the Lord, for his love endures forever."* The story ends by saying, *"As they began to sing and praise, the Lord set ambushes against the men of Ammon and Moab and Mount Seir who were invading Judah, and they were defeated."*

There are so many stories just like this one, such as the one in Acts 16, in which Paul and Silas end up breaking out of jail through their use of praise. Another one can be found in Joshua 6 with walls falling while praise went up in Jericho. God gives but he also loves it when we give to Him. There is a tremendous amount of power wrapped up in the worship we give. Victory will come when you rearm yourself with worship to God. Do not let the devil steal your song. He will try because he knows the power and protection wrapped in it.

Another way to rearm can be found in Ephesians 6:10-14. It tells you that you have entered a new battle with a new enemy. This is a result of your new alignment with the cause of Christ and the cross. It starts off by saying, *"Finally, be strong in the Lord and in his mighty power. Put on the full armor of GOD so that you can take a stand against the devil's schemes. For our struggle is not against flesh and blood, but against the rulers, against the authorities, against the spiritual forces of evil in the heavenly realms. Therefore, put on the full armor of God, so that when the day of evil comes, you may be able to stand your ground, and after you have done everything, to stand. Stand firm then..."* This scripture speaks volumes.

You will be in a battle, but this battle will not be in the natural. It will be against the devil's schemes. What do his schemes look like? We talked about this in the chapter with the cycle of unforgiveness. The enemy schemes to put negative thoughts in our minds that will produce negative emotions and cause us to respond with negative actions. Remember, his whole objective is to kill, steal and destroy. So, tell yourself right now that you must rearm. The definition of rearm is to acquire or build up a new supply of weapons. Get dressed in the armor that God has for you. It will come with His confidence and protection.

Ephesians 6:14 starts off the rearming process with a belt of truth. Truth is the Word of God and with it comes freedom. John 8:23 (NIV) says *"You will know the truth and the knowledge of that truth will set you free."* John 14:6 (NIV) Jesus defines truth for us. He says, *"I am the way and the truth and the life…"* He is the truth so to have him buckled around our waist means we should use the truth the same way a belt is used—to keep us from exposing ourselves to the wrong people and things. When we put a belt around our waist, it is to hold our pants up. The same thing happens with the belt of truth; it helps to hold up the things in our life that need to be held up. We should always seek to speak the truth and hear the truth spoken to us.

This armor is not just for us but for others as well. Truth is something we should always desire to let into our mind, and it should be what we want to put into other people's minds. In a world were gossip and lies are flowing at a rapid rate, we need to be ones that bring the change of flow. Truth brings freedom, and the opposite of truth is a lie, which brings bondage. The devil is the author of all lies. Lies are created to bring destruction. Rearm with truth and watch the beauty and freedom that will come in your pain.

The next piece of the armor that God wants to clothe you with is a breastplate of righteousness. This righteousness is not your own, so don't freak out. Our righteousness is as filthy rags (Isaiah 64:6), but remember this is the Armor of God, not of you. God's righteousness is based on the blood that he shed on the cross. When we understand that our righteousness is filthy, but His is grace, great protection can come.

Again, back to Dylan, my sailor: If his uniform were filthy, it would be a sign of disrespect and dishonor. Before he left for Japan, where he is stationed, we went for a family photo and he had to make sure every wrinkle was removed, and every crease was exact because he did not want to represent this country with lack of effort or laziness.

What we need to understand about the breastplate of righteousness is when we try to walk in our righteousness, we are representing the cross wrong. We are representing with filth like anger, pride, and arrogance. Fountains of Grace come with Christ's righteousness. We place the breastplate over our heart because when we cover ourselves in His righteousness our hearts will beat, and rivers of love and grace will flow from us. Clothe yourself in that righteousness not your own.

Moving along on this journey of armoring up with God's armor, we see the need for our feet being fitted with the readiness that comes from the gospel of peace. Peace is a hot commodity in the world we live in today. We see battles raging all around us. Battles in the country, in families, in schools, and in the world in general. Everyone is looking for the peace to calm the storm. When in a battle of brokenness, the enemy wants us only to see strife, but when we see the beauty in the brokenness, it will bring the peace that passes all understanding.

Do you wonder why we would want this peace fitted on our feet? It is so that we can walk into every battle, every situation and every painful moment with peace knowing that God has us covered. Put the shoes on and armor up to *"Make every effort to live in peace with everyone and be holy; without holiness, no one will see the Lord (Hebrews 12: 14)."*

Next is the shield of faith. There is a lot to say about faith. In reading Hebrews 11, it will give you a clear understanding of what faith is and what it does. It states, *"Faith is being sure of what we hope for and certain of what we do not see (Hebrews 11:1 NIV)."* This scripture goes on to discuss what several people in the Bible did to display their faith.

Hebrews 11:	Person of the Bible	What they did	What their faith produced
3	God	Formed the world	The world
4	Able	Offered a better sacrifice	Hearing the voice of God

5	Enoch	Taken from life and did not experience death	Life pleasing to God
7	Noah	Built an Ark	Inheritance
8	Abraham	Went to a foreign country when told by God to do so	Obedience
11	Abraham and Sarah	Believed for a child past childbearing year	Gave birth
21	Jacob	Blessed his sons	Worship
22	Joseph	Spoke of his end and the exodus	A voice
23	Moses' parents	Hid Moses for three months	Removal of fear
24	Moses	Refused to be known as the son of Pharaoh's daughter, left Egypt, resisted pleasures of sin, kept Passover	Freedom
29	People	Passed through the Red Sea	Promise

30	People marching around Jericho	Marched around Jericho	Walls fell
31	Rahab	Welcomed spies	Salvation

Hebrew 11:32-36 states *"I don't have the time to tell you about Gideon, Barak, Samson, Jephthah, David, Samuel and the prophets, who through faith conquered kingdoms, administered justice, and gained what was promised; who shut the mouths of lions, quenched the fury of flames, and escaped the edge of the sword; whose weakness was turned to strength; and who became powerful in battle and routed foreign armies."* It continues to say that there were some people raised back to life by faith, some were stoned, sawed in two, put to death by the sword, destitute, persecuted, mistreated and some wandered into dessert.

Many horrible situations, situations of brokenness that produced great beauty by faith. It is impossible to please God if we walk in a lack of faith. These great men and women of the Bible pleased God because they were willing and ready to walk with the shield of faith held high. It is noted that this shield of faith will catch every fiery dart that the enemy tries to throw at you. Armor up with faith today and watch the enemy be silenced so that you can raise the victory flag in your life.

You then need to put on your helmet of salvation and take up the sword of the spirit, which is the word of God. When you armor up with the helmet of salvation, you are covering your mind, your eyes, your ears, your mouth and your nose with the salvation. Salvation is an eternity and has so much wrapped in it. Salvation is life. So, when you put that helmet on you are allowing God to create life in your mind, in the words that you speak, in what you see and in words that you hear.

In that same verse, it says to armor up with the sword of the Spirit, which is the word of God. The word of God sets us free. The word of God gives us wisdom. The word of God gives us understanding. The word of God gives us nourishment. The word of God gives us comfort. The word of God gives us peace. The word of God gives us praise. The word of God gives us confirmation. The word of God gives us hope. The word of God gives us light. When you are in an intense battle all the things that the word gives can be used as a sword to slice the enemy's head off and send it back to the pit of hell where it belongs. The sword is vital in this new battle against principalities. You can gain and maintain complete victory when you armor up with the sword of the Spirit.

This scripture goes on to read, *"Pray in the Spirit on all occasions with all kinds of prayers and requests."* When you go to God ask Him to help you walk this journey of being Beautifully Broken, you can take every situation and say…

Death has no victory over me.
Divorce has no victory over me.
Disease has no victory over me.
Depression has no victory over me.
Darkness has no victory over me.
Disability has no victory over me.

Nothing has victory over you when you rearm yourself with the armor of God. You will walk in victory today and every day.

REALITY RECALL

By Jennifer Lee

Life as we knew it was over.

In the early hours of May 4, 2017, our daughter and grandbaby, that our daughter lovingly called "Peanut," were tragically murdered. They were in the wrong place at the wrong time, as stated many times by the police. The day I found out that our daughter and grandbaby were murdered, I began to deal with every emotion you could think of. I became angry, confused, helpless, shattered—just simply broken. I couldn't quite understand what the authorities were saying to me. I kept telling myself repeatedly to wake up from this horrible nightmare that I just could not seem to get out of. No matter what I did, I could not wake up.

A brief time later, I had to face my other three children with the most devastating news of their lives: The news that the life that we always loved is no longer. The little girl they grew up with wasn't coming home anymore. The hardest part as a parent is watching your children hurt and knowing there is nothing you can do to help them.

As I began to watch their hearts unfold in front of my eyes, I just couldn't understand. I felt like I was watching my children through a glass window. I couldn't even reach out and help them. I couldn't even help myself for that matter. Something as simple as lifting my head off the pillow had become too difficult even to accomplish. The same pillow that I had prayed on time and time again was the pillow that I felt like I was dying on. I WAS SIMPLY BROKEN. My thought was: That man didn't just kill my daughter and my grandbaby, he killed my entire family.

Then on August 5, 2017, just a mere 91 days after our daughter's death we got another knock on our door by the authorities. This time it was for our son. The police said, "Your son was in a horrible car accident in which he lost his life." He went home to be with his grandma and sister in heaven. At one of the lowest points in my life, my head hit the floor, and I heard nothing but a voice telling me, "This is the only way." As I looked around, there was no one in the room but me. I heard this voice but was perplexed at where it came from. As I asked, "Why, why me, why them? I've been a good mom. I did my best God; how could you take them from me?" I heard nothing back.

The only thing I kept asking God was, "How long are you going to make me stay here without them?" The days became long, and nights became even longer. Outside my window, the world was still moving, and the lives of everyone around me were still the same, but I was dying on the inside.

A brief time later, things started to happen to me that involved young pregnant girls. I kept asking, "Why, why are they coming around me?" I didn't want to see them. I didn't want them around me. They made me miss her more, and that same voice that I heard on the floor after my son's death said, "This is the why." "WHAT?" I screamed out, "What does this mean?" It was at this moment I got a vision of a home I had put together for young pregnant girls. This home would be a rescue home for pregnant teens. It would be designed to help them get out of trouble and into a productive environment.

When you lose a child, you have two options. You either lay there and stay numb or tell your heart to beat again. On that Sunday morning, I knew it was time for me to get right with GOD. I know the ONE that has my children and "The One" who has been speaking to me: It is God. From that day forward, I decided that I had to live because my other two children needed me, and I needed them. I had to make sure that my children that were now in heaven lived through me and that their story would be heard in order to bring change and hope to others.

Shortly after this encounter, I found out that the man that killed our daughter received a charge of murder for her and only aggravated battery for our grandbaby. This created a passion inside of me for justice. In Indiana, they do not consider a baby inside of the womb a baby, which meant that the murderer would not be charged for my grandbaby's death. I began to feel Jesus ignite a passion inside of me. I began to feel myself come alive again. I told my family I would fight this law for my grandbaby until I couldn't fight it anymore. I wanted justice for Peanut. My grandbaby was planned, loved and already had put imprints on many hearts. How dare they not consider our little Peanut a baby.

So, the fight began, with GOD on our side and everything in me I fought hard. The victory came approximately a year later; the state of Indiana now has a law called the "Brittney and Peanut law." This law doesn't go for our little Peanut, but it will go for the next man or woman that decides to commit a senseless act on a pregnant woman.

As I began to put all my focus on changing this law, things began happening to me. Young moms kept running through my head. I prayed about it repeatedly. That same voice said, "This is the way."

I started a non-profit Christian program called *Hope for Peanut*. It provides an opportunity for pregnant mothers to choose life by being a positive support system for them during the pregnancy and the months following the delivery. I want to help them build their inner strength so that they can reach their full potential as mothers. I want to help them heal from their pasts, so they can move forward to become independent adults and amazing parents along the way. The idea is to support the residents physically, emotionally, and spiritually in every way. I believe this is God's plan to bring peace to my heart. Only God can turn a mess into a message, a test into a testimony, a trial into a triumph, a victim into a victory and a bunch of fragmented pieces into something beautiful. ROMANS 8:28 (NIV) *"And we know that in all things God works for the good of those who love Him, who have been called according to His purpose."*

You can visit the Hope for Peanut website to gain more information or offer support for the ministry at www.hopeforpeanut.org

MEDITATION MOMENT

STILL MOMENT

Sit still for a few minutes and let God fill you full of faith and encouragement while you rest in all that He has given and did to protect you.

PRAYER
God,

I pray and put on your full armor. I start from the top of my head and work to the soles of my feet. There is not an ounce of me that you do not cover when I armor up with your gear. So right now, I put on the helmet of salvation that will protect my mind, protect my vision, protect my mouth and my ears. God, I want to hear, see, confess and think on all that you are. I put on the breastplate of righteousness; it is not my righteousness but yours that causes my heart to be protected. I put on the belt of truth that allows me to speak your truth today and hear your truth that is spoken to me. Make me aware and alert to all lies that the enemy may try to throw my way. I put your peace on my feet. Help me to walk into every situation today with the peace of who you are. I want to carry the peace that passes all understanding everywhere my feet may step. I take up the shield of faith that will catch every fiery dart that the enemy may try to throw at me. Help me to continuously understand and dwell in your faith that brings so many remarkable things in my life, not just for me but others. I take up the sword, which is your word, and confess it all day to destroy the enemy's lies in my life. God help me today to pray in all situations and have faith to move mountains.

In Jesus' name, amen.

WORD

You may be thinking like Jennifer was and like most of the recall stories that the authors have confessed, asking, "GOD, why?" You may be in the stage of asking how a loving God could do this to anyone or allow this to happen. When broken, we commonly ask this question.

In the book of Exodus, it lays it out clearly why these things happen and why God allows it. Open your Bible to the story of Moses found in Exodus 10 (NIV). God is bringing the plagues on to the Egyptians. He tells Moses to return to Pharaoh and make his demands again. He wanted Moses to tell him to let his people go. God says *"I have made him and his officials stubborn so that I can display my miraculous signs among them. I've also done it so you can tell your children and grandchildren about how I made a mockery of the Egyptians and about the signs I displayed among them and so you will know that I am the Lord."*

You can see in this portion of scripture that God walks us through brokenness for four reasons. 1) The world can see His miraculous signs; 2) So that generations will know about how great God is; 3) To display signs among all people, and 4) So that the world and generations will know that He is Lord. Let Him illuminate through you to the world so that greatness can come for generations.

WORSHIP

Listen to the song "This Is How I Fight My Battles" by Upper Room. Know that it doesn't matter what battle you fight; you can win in worship. When you lift God up above your brokenness, He will get the glory in your situations.

LINK LEVERAGE TOOL

AWARENESS
- Write three words that stood out to you while reading this chapter.

ASK
- Ask yourself what did these words speak to you?

GOAL
- Write down one goal that will help you to grow this week.

CHANGE
- What change can you make to acheive your goal?

SERVE
- Who did I serve this week and how did it make me feel?

ILLUMINATION

Use this journal to write three valuable nuggets that you learned in this chapter and how you have won in life because of them. Then write three things you are thankful for. Look for the light in your darkness.

_____
_____
_____
_____
_____
_____
_____
_____
_____
_____
_____
_____
_____
_____
_____
_____
_____
_____
_____
_____
_____
_____
_____
_____
_____

Armor up so that you can be victorious in this new battle for your soul and future

Use this page to draw what is on your mind, write out scriptures that stand out or quotes that speak to you.

STEP 8
RECIPROCATE THE ILLUMINATION

Don't give up on you because God will never give up on you.

AFRESH

Have you ever given and given to someone and never received anything in return? This can clog up a desire to give. Have you ever had the friend that gives the greatest gifts and you do not know how to respond to their giving? This is how you may have felt while walking through this process. When God is done walking you through a journey of healing you may look back at all that he has done and say, "God, how can I repay you?" Everyone thinks that God gives freely without expecting any reciprocation, but I beg to differ. Jesus gave us a great commission—He said, "I want you to reciprocate what I have given you by you giving it to the world."

Reciprocate means to give and take. Throughout this book, your journey and throughout the rest of your life, you will take from God. You will take the breath He gives until He gives it no more, you will take the sight He gives until He gives it no more, you will take the freedom He gives, and you will take the light He gives. The question is, do we reciprocate that back? God says the way to give back to him is to become the illumination in and to the world.

In Matthew 5 it starts off with Jesus telling everyone that He wants to give to us. It says: *"If you are poor in spirit, I will give you the kingdom of heaven. If you are mourning, I will give you comfort. If you are meek, I will give you the earth. If you hunger and thirst after righteousness, I fill you with righteousness. If you are merciful, I will give you mercy. If you are pure in heart, I will let you see me. If you are a peacemaker, I will call you the children of God. If you are persecuted for righteousness, then I will give you the kingdom of heaven. If people insult you, persecute you and say all kinds of evil against you because of me, then great is your reward in heaven."*

Jesus has a lot that he wants to give us. It seems like, in every broken situation, He is ready to reciprocate in our brokenness.

However, he will want a return for His giving. Immediately following these verses Jesus says, *"You are the salt of the earth..."* then in verse 14 He tells us, *"You are the light now to the world."* He goes on to explain a town built on a hill cannot be hidden.

It makes me think of a time when I graduated with my bachelor's degree. Me, my son, son-in-law and daughter went to Lynchburg, Virginia to the Liberty University campus for my ceremony. When we were leaving, my son, Daniel, said, "I want to take you somewhere." It was a star on top of Mill Mountain in Roanoke, Virginia. We arrived right before darkness came. He wanted me to see it in the daylight and at night. At night it sat upon a high hill but brought light to the whole community around it. It was amazing! They say the star is used as a beacon to welcome the visitors that come.

This is a real-life example of what God is talking about in Matthew. We are a city on a hill that cannot be hidden. As we drove down the hill, we could see the light for miles and miles. This was a city on a hill that could not be hidden because of the light that was being displayed for all to see. We are the light of the world. It is time to illuminate. It is time to shine into the dark places of the world.

In our brokenness, we often say there is so much darkness, how can my light make a difference? It is not about your light but about the one who gave you the light. The light does not come from us but the creator of light. In Genesis 1, one of the very first things God spoke into existence was light. He said in verse 3, *"Let there be light"* and guess what happened? There was light. God spoke light into your life through the Word.

If we go back to Matthew 5, Jesus is referring to us as a lamp. He says, *"Do people light a lamp and put it under a bowl."* We cannot hide what God has done for us as we have walked through this entire process. You may not feel like you are walking in complete victory because the completeness comes when you walk out of this part of the process. It is when you give back to God what he has given to you that things become complete.

Think for a minute all that He has given to you on the journey through this book?

- In the RECOGNITION of the beauty, He gave you your thoughts back.

- In the RECALL of the moments, He gave you your voice back.

- In the REVIVAL of your Heart, He gave your love back.

- In the RECEIVING the Fountains of Grace, He gave you your faith back.

- In the RESPOND to the Strip Down, He gave you your peace back.

- In the REALIGNMENT, He gave you your connections back.
- In the REARMING, He gave you your fight back.
- In the RECIPROCATION of the Illumination, He is going to give you your vision back.

You have a purpose in this world, and it is to be the light. The light was created for a specific purpose. What is your specific purpose for being here on this earth? I felt like I had no life left in me because I thought that God could not use me ever again due to my failures. I thought that I was trash and had no purpose. It was when I allowed myself to see again that I began to shine again. Where there is no vision, people will perish—they die. Suicide happens when people just cannot see their future purpose or even the purpose for their now. So, let's take a journey through discovering what it is you are called to do.

Understand first how our eyes work. How do we see things in the natural? The American Optometric Association says that it is all about the light. You can only see an object when the light rays reflect off that object. They go on to talk about the cones, rods, iris, and pupils, which I will spare you of the details. However, the discussion is all about the eyes reflecting this light, and the light changing the shape of things and opening and closing parts of the eye itself. It is all about the light. When you can see, the illumination will begin.

It is time to run out of the grave of darkness that has trapped you in negative emotions, thoughts, and actions and step into the light and experience the restored vision. Darkness destroys vision, destiny, and lives. We were wonderfully and fearfully made by Christ. Christ knitted and stitched us for a purpose and our time is NOW.

What will you do with the light? Will you hide it under a shade of pain or use it to bring light to all the lives you encounter? The word promises that God will take every situation and turn it into something glorious for his namesake. It is not time to shrink back into the pattern of destruction but to settle in the pattern of light that will cause you to see again. What dreams have died because you haven't seen the Beauty in your Brokenness?

_____
_____
_____
_____
_____

    I was a youth pastor, and in my brokenness, I withdrew from that calling. I quit working with children and teens and settled into the darkness of doing my own thing. It was not until I stepped back that I realized I had stopped seeing because I stopped believing God could. When we withdraw from God, we start believing the lies or the myths about the visions God gives us. God gives us a vision and we say, "God, I can't" because:

- **I am too broken**- If this is an accurate statement then why did God use so many messed up people in the Bible? Each person used in a mighty way worked their way through their moments of brokenness to see vision and illumination.

- **I am too young**- Study Daniel and see how old he was in the Bible. He was said to be a young teenager but brought the light of God's great protection for the world to see. We are still talking about him thousands of years later.

- **I am too old**- Think about Abraham and Sarah—they were each over 100 years old when they gave birth to the promise from God. They helped the world become illuminated with the idea of faith and commitment to the promises of God.

- **I am to poor**- There is a story in the gospels that Jesus presents of a woman defined as a poor widow. Jesus is watching a bunch of rich people throw gifts into the temple treasure (offering plate). He then sees the widow throw all that she had on the plate. He tells everyone this woman gave more because she gave out of her need. She gave it all. A requirement to be used by God is to be willing to give it all.

We can make up excuses and continue to walk in them, or we can break out of the excuses and allow the illumination to bring us vision. God says in the Message version of Proverbs 29:18, *"If people can't see what God is doing, they stumble all over themselves; but when they attend to what he reveals, they are most blessed."* It is also stated in Proverbs that as you delight in him (the light), He will give you the desires of your heart. This is because He is the one that is dwelling in your heart and your desires become His desires for you. What is your heart desiring right now?

_____

_____

Do not search your heart and see that the desires are too big and withdraw. This is what I did regarding authoring this book. English is my worst subject. I am sure as you have read this you have found grammatical errors even after several editors have viewed it. But God, He can move all our insecurities, failures and weaknesses into greatness as we surrender to Him. I sat on this vision for almost two years. Until one day, I decided that it was in the dark and I needed to bring it to the light. I went to Florida for a month and focused on the completing this book.
What vision did God give you that you need to quit sitting on?

_____

_____

Israelmore Ayivar of Leaders Watchwords says, "The kind of death you should mourn over is the one that happens when you abort your potentials prematurely!" Life without purpose is a tragedy. Begin to see the purpose and vision for your life again. Bring triumph out of your tragedy and let the world be illuminated by the beauty in your brokenness. It is in that moment that all who see the light will get their vision back.

Do you know what God wants you to do to turn your pain into purpose? Here is an exercise for you to do and discuss with your Link partner.

Draw a big circle in the center of a piece of paper.

1. Pray and let God know you are ready to illuminate, and you need direction from Him.
2. Remember the recall of your story.
3. Remember the brokenness in the recall—what made you cry the most about it.
4. Remember the beauty in the recall—what brought you to the place of joy.
5. Remember the illumination in the recall—what can you use about your situation to bring light to other people that may be walking a similar journey.

Just to show you how it worked for me:

RECIPROCATE THE ILLUMINATION

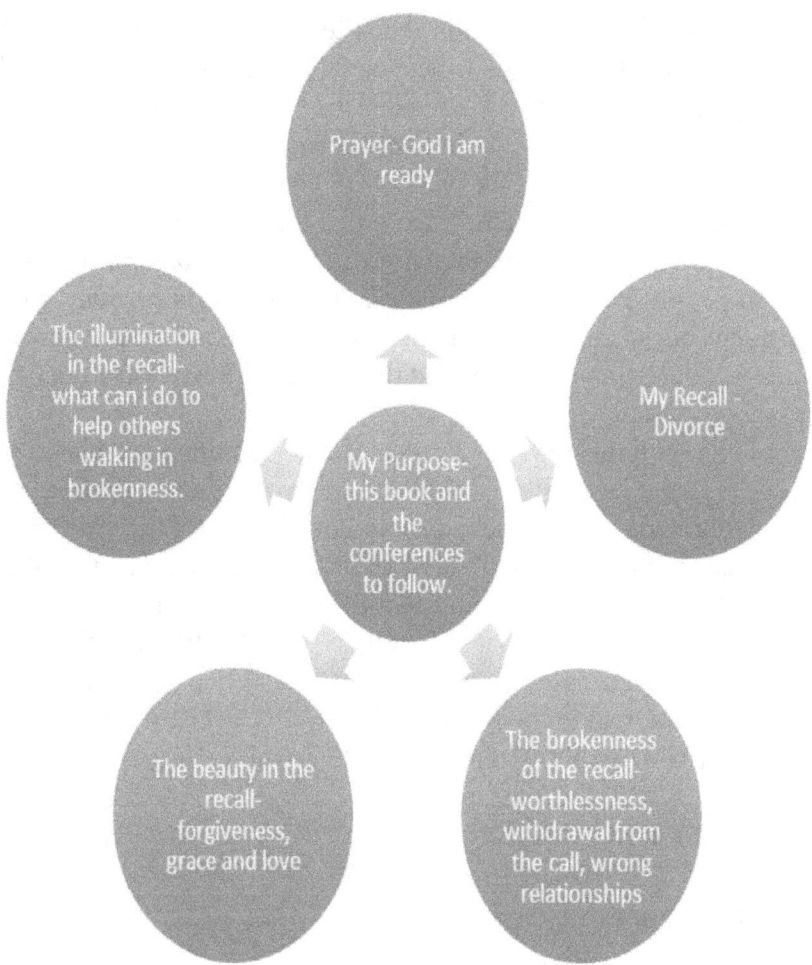

Sometimes people will ask you what your strengths and weakness are, but I have found that it doesn't matter. Remember God says, *"In weakness, He will be made strong."* 2 Corinthians 12:9. Philippians 4:13 tell us that we *"can do all things through Christ who strengthens* us." It is not our natural strength that leads us to the purpose. It is the supernatural strength that leads us there.

Dream God's dreams for your life. God's dreams are so big that we cannot accomplish them without His assistance and full involvement. That is why this step is the last step. You had to walk through the process of getting connected to the light so that you could see the objects of the dreams God has for you with clarity.

Now back to Matthew 5 again this time we will start at verse 16, *"In the same way let your light shine before others, that they may see your good deeds and glorify your father in heaven."* The vision is big so that you will glorify the one who is bigger than you. This is not about you! It is about the reciprocation of what the light giver gave you.

Let your light shine before men. Create a return in exchange for what you received. How would you like your life to be different a year from today? It is time to dance again. Time to dance with your dreams and stop stuffing them in the trash. You have walked through a process of learning that there is beauty in every bit of your brokenness. So, what will you do with that beauty? Will you throw it away, hide it, destroy it or live it? When you live it, you begin to be a light to the world. YOU BEGIN TO RECIPROCATE THE ILLUMINATION THAT CHRIST GAVE YOU.

REALITY RECALL

By Cheri Gable

I was in a season of doing my own thing, and I had withdrawn from my call to youth ministry. I was a youth pastor for 14 years when I began to walk through a season of what I felt like was abandonment. I felt like God and many people had abandoned me. I did not want anything to do with God. I thought that God had failed me, and I had failed him too much to ever do anything for him again. I had this false perception that God could never use me to fulfill anything because I was a broken, hot mess. But God, when

I allowed Him to step into my brokenness, helped me to see the beauty in it all.

I was in my room crying hysterically because I felt like such a failure. As I laid there crying into my pillow my son heard me. He walked in and said, "Mom what is wrong?" He was 21-years-old, so I felt I could share with him. I told him I was overcome by the feeling that I was a failure. He laid over me and stretched his arms from my head to my toes and began to pray. At that moment he said, "Mom I feel like God has closed one door to open another one for you."

You hear those words all the time, so at that moment it didn't bring me peace. However, two days later we attended a church in Fishers, Indiana called ITOWN. It was in that moment that what my son spoke to me came to life. The pastor was preaching a series called "DOORS." The pastor began to preach, and he started off with a scripture found in Revelation 3:7 *"...The Holy, the True-David's key in his hand, opening doors no one can lock, locking doors no one can open- speaks:"* The pastor began to talk about God doing a new thing, and He was not finished with us yet.

This day started the process of vision coming to life and light beginning to shine from me again. I began to illuminate. Let God speak vision to you today and allow yourself to begin to understand that God can use you. Don't be afraid to dream again. Don't give up on you because God will never give up on you. He will continuously pursue you because he knows and understands that there is greatness in you! He knows you can change the world. This book is a result of a vision that God gave me. This was not something that had crossed my mind. But God, he gives you a vision that will be way bigger than you so that you don't get any credit for it. He wants all the glory for the visions that He gives. Know that God wants you to have big dreams, plans, and solutions. Do not stay stuck in the darkness of your story. Know that Christ wants to illuminate you to a place of victory and cause you to shine.

MEDITATION MOMENT

STILL MOMENT

Sit still for several moments and think about all the blessings in your life, both big and small. Let your mind dwell on God's goodness to you and how you can use it to bring life and joy to others.

PRAYER
God,

Help me see again, help me to live again and to give again. I want to know exactly how you would have me illuminate your love, peace, and grace to the world. Open doors of opportunity for me to serve. Create divine appointments for me to pour beauty into others. Shine your favor on me so that others can gain from my story. I know that you do not walk us through any situation without a victory coming in the end. You turn all bad into good for your glory. God, I humble myself so that you can get the glory for everything that you call me to do. I give you the spotlight—it is not my light that I want to illuminate this world with. I want it to be your light; the light that lights up all paths that lead to you. Your Word is a lamp unto my feet and a light unto my path, so reignite me, God. Put your oil in my lamp and cause me to burn for you.

In Jesus' name, amen.

WORD

There is a song called "Alabaster Box" by Cece Winans. It is all about a story from the word about a woman caught in sin but willing to bust through all shame, misconceptions, and failures to get to Jesus. The woman in the song comes from Luke 7:36-50. Jesus is invited to a house of a Pharisee to recline at his table. While

Jesus is sitting there, a sinful woman enters in with an alabaster box of perfume. She quietly sits at Jesus' feet and begins to wash his feet with her tears, and she dries the tears with her hair. She then begins to kiss his feet. The Pharisee that had invited Jesus said, *"If you only knew who was kissing your feet."* He started pointing his finger at her and calling her out. Jesus, being the gentlemen that he is, started telling the man, *"You do not understand. I walked in here, and you did nothing for me. This woman walks in and makes an outward display of her love and gratitude for me."* Jesus tells the Pharisee that *"Those who are forgiven of little love little but those forgiven of much love much."* Jesus then tells the woman, *"Your faith has healed you, go in peace."* Jesus was telling the woman that she's now illuminated and to carry his light to the world. This woman did not let anything stop her from getting to the one that she could receive the oil from. She pressed through the insecurities caused by her shame, the fear caused by her lack of faith, and the failure caused by her brokenness. Be like this woman and press through to get the oil that you can pour out to others and ignite their lamps that have gone out so that they can illuminate.

WORSHIP

Reciprocate the illumination NOW! Listen to Toby Mac's "Let Your Light Shine." This is all about letting your light shine bright everywhere you go.

It's time...
TIME TO ILLUMINATE IN YOUR BROKENNESS!

Remember that this is not the end. You will walk through situations that break you again.
Use these steps to refresh your memory when you lose site of the great BEAUTY IN YOUR BROKEN.

LINK LEVERAGE TOOL

AWARENESS
- Write three words that stood out to you while reading this chapter.

ASK
- Ask yourself what did these words speak to you?

GOAL
- Write down one goal that will help you to grow this week.

CHANGE
- What change can you make to acheive your goal?

SERVE
- Who did I serve this week and how did it make me feel?

ILLUMINATION

Use this journal to write three valuable nuggets that you learned in this chapter and how you have won in life because of them. Then write three things you are thankful for. Look for the light in your darkness.

_____
_____
_____
_____
_____
_____
_____
_____
_____
_____
_____
_____
_____
_____
_____
_____
_____
_____
_____
_____
_____
_____
_____
_____

You have a purpose in this world; it is to be the light.

About the author:

I am an avid traveler and just last year visited 6 countries and 12 different states. I also enjoy nature, adventure, meeting new people, exploring new cultures and sharing my faith with the world. I am a divorced mother of three successful children and one beautiful, energetic grandchild. I went back to college in my 40's while working full time to get a master's degree in human service with a focus on life coaching, a bachelor's degree in science religion and a minor in business.

I have coached students and families for 20+ years and have a lifelong vision to guide all people into uniting their passion to their purpose and guiding them to fulfilling their destiny. I have a deep burning in my heart to flip the script on "hurting people hurt people." I want people to see that there is great beauty in all the situations they walk through and help them fulfill the purpose that God has put them on this earth to achieve.

For more information on the author, for life coaching or for conference dates please go to:
W: https://bb.life/
E: Beautifullybroken@bb.life
P: 317-989-0022

IT IS YOUR TIME TO SHINE!

www.ingramcontent.com/pod-product-compliance
Lightning Source LLC
Chambersburg PA
CBHW071404290426
44108CB00014B/1684